The Comedy of Survival

The Comedy of Survival

LITERARY ECOLOGY AND A PLAY ETHIC

Joseph W. Meeker

Third Edition

The University of Arizona Press * *Tucson*

The University of Arizona Press
© 1997 Joseph W. Meeker

⊗ This book is printed on acid free, archival-quality paper.
Manufactured in the United States of America

02 01 00 99 98 97   6 5 4 3 2 1

Library of Congress Cataloging-in-Publication Data

Meeker, Joseph W.
The comedy of survival: literary ecology and a play ethic /
Joseph W. Meeker.—3rd ed.
p.   cm.
Includes bibliographical references and index.
ISBN 0-8165-1685-5 (cloth : alk. paper).—ISBN 0-8165-1686-3
(paper : alk. paper)
1. Human ecology in literature.   I. Title.
PN48.M4   1997
809'.93355—dc21   97-4812
        CIP

British Library Cataloging-in-Publication Data
A catalogue record for this book is available from the British Library.

For Helen Meeker,

 Wife and Playmate,

And Midwife to

 This our Offspring

Contents

Preface

Some books, like some people, have several careers in the course of their lives. This one has taken decades deciding what it wants to be. It began when I was asked to say a few words about comedy at a college drama awards ceremony in 1969. Over the next few years it became a complex research project that took me to several European countries and required the integration of fieldwork in wildlife ecology with scholarship in comparative literature. The result was a book called *The Comedy of Survival: Studies in Literary Ecology* (New York: Charles Scribner's Sons, 1974). Some people loved the book, others despised it (one reviewer suggested that all copies should be burned), and many were indifferent to it.

Yet it retained enough interest that a new edition seemed to be called for by 1980. Revisions were made to bring the text up to date, new illustrations by wildlife artist Bill Berry were added, and the new title was *The Comedy of Survival: In Search of an Environmental Ethic* (Los Angeles: Guild of Tutors Press, 1980). This edition has been hobbling along since, appearing as a college text now and then, and finding its way into both scholarship and the public mind. During that time, people have become more aware that human culture and artistic creations are central to our influences upon natural environments. Now it is no longer strange to hear that the natural world is a positive source of energy and ideas, and that our best role on the planet may be in finding ways to participate in natural processes without insisting that we manage all of them. Collectively, we have matured to the point where we may be able to take comedy seriously.

I am no longer the person I was when I began this endeavor. I have learned much, and lost a few things. The important learning has come through the study of systemic relationships in nature through the growth of chaos theory and complex dynamics. These hold the promise of reintroducing poetic thinking into scientific research, and banishing the oversimple mechanistic models that have made science so dull and cloddish over the past three centuries. Other new learning has come through the investigation of play, and the discovery that the comic spirit expresses itself in play throughout human life and among many other species of animals. Play is itself a complex system that no one now fully understands, and it will remain a mystery deserving inquiry for decades to come.

The things I have lost are mostly good riddance. I no longer have academic ambitions, so I don't need to try to impress colleagues with my erudition and scholarship. I can speak in my own voice, and forget about the distant anonymity that once characterized academic prose. I can tell stories rather than merely multiplying footnotes when I want to illustrate a point. In short, some of the shackles of mid-career restraint have fallen away, and I no longer care so much what others may think. The regret that comes with growing older is softened by the joy of increased freedoms.

Friends and colleagues have given much to help this book grow. Konrad Lorenz gave me the first assurance I needed, and this was strengthened by the help of Sir Frank Fraser Darling and Arne Naess. Paul Sheperd understood at once, and encouraged me at every step. From Stuart Brown I learned about play, and from Brian Swimme and Thomas Berry about cosmic play. My wife Helen has been a constant well of love and understanding, and a dependable source of intelligent advice. I am deeply grateful to these people, and to the many others who have responded in positive and negative ways that have made it possible for this book to discover its identity.

So let us play together in the comic way.

The Comedy of Survival

1 * Introduction to Literary Ecology

Meeting new people, in most traditional cultures, is an occasion for telling stories about ancestors. As you and I become acquainted, let me say a few words about my folks.

Sinus Block sounds like a nasal problem, but it was also the name of my maternal grandfather. He came to America from Germany as a boy of twelve in 1884, and grew up in an almost archetypal immigrant story: during his youth he was a farm laborer with no schooling, he saved money to buy a small furniture business, married an immigrant woman who bore him three children, and by midlife, now a mortician, was one of the wealthiest men in Waterloo, Iowa, a pillar of his church, and a bigot. Sinus lived until I was in my mid-twenties, but I think we never had a conversation, just the two of us. He was stern, distant, evidently uninterested in young people. I don't have a single personal story that I can tell about Sinus Block, although there is some interesting family lore about the severe life that he lived.

Joseph Meeker sounds like me, but it was also the name of my father's father. His ancestors had been in America for a long time, since their first arrival in New Jersey from England in 1635. From that time until Joe Meeker was forced to sell his Iowa farm during the economic crash of 1929, all Meekers had been farmers. Since then, none have been. Joe died when I was only five years old, so I have few personal memories of him, but even so I feel that I know him closely. He was a musician and an armchair philosopher, as were all ten of his children. Music, spirited argumentation, and storytelling filled the house whenever I visited, before and after grandfather's death. In the photos I have of him, he shows a wry smile under a shock of unruly white hair, and he holds a fiddle.

Two generations later, these two genetic and cultural traditions are mingled in me, and they have something to do with my reasons for writing this book. The Sinus Block in my life tries to simplify things into polarized forms of good and evil, black and white, for and against. He is interested in controlling people and events around him, and it is important to him that he feel powerful. He is politically conservative, and wealth is an important part of his self-image, as well as a weapon of defense and attack. Life seems like a contest to him, and he is determined to win. I see him with his fist clenched and his jaw set.

Grandpa Joe's chin rests on his violin, and his fingers are busy making music. Grandpa Joe never managed to do anything that was good for business. He was, by all accounts, a mediocre farmer who failed to put in the eighteen-hour days required for success. Joe seems to have been interested in his family, and in music. Politically, he styled himself a socialist, and revered Eugene V. Debs, who preached the dignity of poverty and the evils of wealth. After World War I, Joe organized his family into The Meeker Orchestra, in which all of his children played the instruments he had taught them, and they traveled the muddy roads of Iowa to play at dances and concerts. Keeping this family together was the main reason for working the farm, and Joe devised a scheme to buy enough land so that all could work and live together in his idea of a musical, socialist, familial Utopia. The large debt required to establish such an empire was what made the farm vulnerable at the financial collapse of 1929. When the farm was sold by the bank, the family dispersed and Joe's dream dissolved.

As I feel these grandfathers within me, I know that they represent many centuries of cultural and genetic tradition, and that their differing behavior and values are not merely of their own making. Their patterns of character and temperament are to be found in the literatures of many cultures over the past six thousand years of recorded history, and even more profoundly in the traditions of oral mythology. People, and other animals as well, live by patterns of behavior that have evolved over many millions of years.

Evidence helpful toward understanding the varieties of behavior comes from several sources. One of my favorite sources is literary art, where gifted writers have provided detailed accounts of behavior, motives, and settings from every culture and period of the past. Another good source is scientific ethology, the detailed study of animal behavior, and its recent extension into evolutionary psychology, the study of genetic bases for behavior. In the coming pages, I will try to bring together insights from the study of literature and from the biological sciences in search of patterns that may help us understand human relationship to our various pasts, both evolutionary and cultural.

Sinus Block, for instance, may be best illuminated by examining cultural history. He was born in a small town on Germany's North Sea. For centuries, this area has been the home of Teutonic Knights, Prussian militarism, vigorous commercial enterprise, Protestant religious fanaticism, and the power politics of the Hanseatic League. Rigidity of personal character and of social structure are commonplace there. Power, control, and sharply polarized thinking were no doubt in the air as Sinus grew up, and it was the same air he brought with him to the German community in Iowa. But Germany did not invent these patterns of behavior, for there are strong traces of them in ancient Greece as well, and a fairly continuous line of cultural inheritance linking Greece to modern Western nations. Later in this book, I will follow some of these threads by examining the tradition of literary tragedy in Western culture.

Understanding Grandpa Joe will be far more complex. Much of his behavior appears to be purposeless, with no clear goals and no notable record of achievements. Keeping things going from day to day seems to have been enough to satisfy him, until the economy crashed and made even that impossible. Conversation and storytelling required much of his time, but he never earned a dime from them. The Meeker Orchestra charged one dollar admission when they performed for public dances, but that seldom paid their travel costs, and never produced a profit. Music and conversation were both ways to keep family members in touch and cooperating, and Grandpa Joe valued that. His neighbors, I imagine, didn't take him very seriously, for he seemed to be merely playing with his life. I think that's just what he was doing, and I believe that the pattern of his life rests upon an evolutionary antiquity that goes back to the origin of birds and mammals. This pattern, which I call The Comic Way, is the major subject of this book. I will explore it through literary comedy, human and animal play, and the normal behavior of many healthy species.

Literary Ecology

Human beings are the Earth's only literary creatures. Lacking the plants' talent for photosynthesis and unable to fly like birds, humans are yet able to create great epic poems and mediocre office memos, thanks to the peculiar development of their brains. It is generally assumed that this unique literary talent bestows upon humanity a special dignity not enjoyed by other animals. Whooping cranes, were they blessed with self-consciousness, might feel the same about their sophisticated mating rituals. Like us, they might translate their specific peculiarities into status symbols affirming their worth in the world. We would laugh at them, for in honest moments we know well enough that uniqueness does not in itself confer superiority.

If the creation of literature is an important characteristic of the human species, it should be examined carefully and honestly to discover its influence upon human behavior and the natural environment, and to determine what role, if any, it plays in the welfare and survival of humanity, and what insight it offers into human relationships with other species and with the world around us. Is it an activity that adapts us better to life on Earth, or one that sometimes estranges us from life? From the unforgiving perspective of evolution and natural selection, does literature contribute more to our survival than it does to our extinction? Such questions are perhaps no more answerable than those concerning dignity and status, but they may at least lead to new insight rather than to an increase of traditional human anthropocentric smugness. This book will explore these questions in search of links between literature and the phenomena of nature.

As an evolutionary experiment, human consciousness and its systems of literary notation are too recent to judge with much confidence. Perhaps ten thousand years of accumulated human thought, only some six thousand in written records, constitutes slim evidence for evaluating the importance of an evolutionary innovation. What evidence there is, moreover, seems contradictory or uncertain. The unusual human brain has permitted human adaptation to every known natural environment, and manipulation of those environments where human adaptation is marginal. It has led to the domestication of plants and animals on a large scale, thus allowing for rapid population growth and for the development of cities and civilizations. It has created tools to extend human bodily powers, and technologies to organize those tools. It has produced painting, sculpture, music, religion, philosophy, and literature. The activity of the human brain has also brought about the extinction of many animal species and the wholesale disruption of ecosystems on a worldwide scale. It seems capable of destroying most of what it has created and much that it has not.

Considering the evolutionary novelty of consciousness, one would expect to find many false starts and mistakes in these years of early development. How many millions of disasters and millions of years were required to develop successful wings for birds or useful protective coloring for small mammals and insects? The human mind deserves at least as much margin for error as these inventions. Meanwhile we must live with its mistakes, some of which are very costly.

The origins of environmental crisis lie deep in human cultural traditions at levels of human mentality that have remained nearly unchanged for several thousand years. The premises upon which our culture has been built are powerful and durable, and their weight upon us must be appreciated before we can hope to alter their structure. How can our culture change the influence of Homer or Aristotle or Moses or Sophocles upon all that follows from them, including ways of thinking and the inherited images that unconsciously influence human actions and choices? The problem may be of this magnitude. Given such depth, it is possible that "solutions" are more than can be hoped for. Humanity may have to settle for the distinction of being the first species ever to understand the causes of its own extinction. That would be no small accomplishment.

Industry, technology, the exploitation of the Earth and the aggrandizement of humanity are governed by ideas, faith, and mythology. The cultural images describing what we might be have helped us to become what we are: however the human mind imagines the world, that is how the world tends to become for humans. If we think of the Earth as a farm, then we behave as if it were one; if we imagine that the Earth is a spaceship, then we manipulate and direct its path toward our chosen goal. Human mentality is applied to the Earth according to the model we have adopted to explain it to ourselves. Consciousness perpetuates such potent images, transposing them into new contexts and reinterpreting their meaning from generation to generation. That is what a cultural tradition does, and our institutions exist in order to pass such models along. Education acquaints each new generation with the models of life and thought available from previous generations. A crisis of consciousness occurs when there is a widespread recognition that many important models of reality inherited from the human past are inadequate, irrelevant, or destructive when applied to present circumstances.

Intentionally or accidentally, literature has been a major source of the models used to perpetuate our past. Writers are only rarely professors or preachers, and few of them seem to expect that their works will be applied to their readers' experience: Goethe was astonished when lovesick young men flocked to commit suicide in imitation of his sorrowful Werther. Some authors have recognized the tendency to imitate literary models and have taken pains to describe its attendant perils: Dante describes the sufferings in Hell of Paolo and Francesca, who arrived at adultery by reading Arthurian romances; Cervantes attributes Don Quixote's anachronistic career to his reading of books on knight-errantry; and Flaubert explains how Madame Bovary's life was ruined by the influence of romantic novels.

Literary success also condemns works of art to inclusion in academic curricula where they become parts of our "cultural heritage." Academic people often see their task in life as the application of literary and mythological models to contemporary existence. Like most other readers, they look to literature for guidance in the conduct and interpretation of human affairs. Whatever an artist's intentions may have been, his or her works are likely to become models, doctrines, or ideologies once they are incorporated into the educational curriculum of a cultural tradition.

Literature expresses deep human needs and represents the forms of behavior peculiar to a consciousness-bearing animal. It is not primarily a medium of communication or an educational instrument for perpetuating certain kinds of behavior, but it is often treated as if it were both. Because of its relative permanence, literature can be interpreted as if it were a philosophical statement and used as a model to influence the lives of subsequent human generations. Consciously and unconsciously, people imitate literary characters and often try to create in their own lives the circumstances depicted in literature or the motivations that produce its events. Literature that provides models of human relationships with nature may thus influence both human perceptions of nature and human responses to it.

Ecology is an ancient theme in art and literature, however new it may be as a science. Plants, animals, mountains, seas, and sky have traditionally been represented in literature as components of a complete and integrated system in which human beings find or create their proper places. Major literary works also resemble ecosystems in that they present a large and complex panorama of experience in which the relationships of humans to one another are frequently represented in the context of human relationships to nature and its intricate parts. Imagery describing human life is often drawn from biological sources, with people compared to plants and animals and human characteristics defined by reference to natural elements. Further, a literary work is generally based upon a set of ideological assumptions—usually derived from the artist's contemporary culture, although often in conflict with it—that identifies certain principles of nature and defines human relationships to these principles. And perhaps the most pervasive theme, running through the literatures of all cultures and periods, is that of humanity's role in the structure of the world as a whole. Biological nature is often the image of this larger world.

Literary Ecology, then, is the study of biological themes and relationships that appear in literary works. It is simultaneously an attempt to discover what roles literature has played in the ecology of the human species. Many intellectual disciplines must contribute to the study of literary ecology. Literary form must be reconciled if possible with the forms and structures of nature as they are defined by scientific ecologists, for both are related to human perceptions of beauty and balance. Characters in literature may also be analyzed as typical or atypical representatives of the human species, and their behavior compared to patterns of behavior among other animals as described by contemporary ethology. Philosophical ideas defining the relationship between humanity and nature are often expressed or implied in literary works, revealing a history of human beliefs about the meaning of natural processes, and also revealing the cultural ideologies that have contributed to the modern ecological crisis. Finally, literary ecology makes it possible to study the function of literary art as it influences the survival and well-being of the human species.

Recent years have seen a surge of academic interest in making connections between environmental studies and literary criticism. There are new professional organizations and journals of literary ecology, and recent books exploring relationships between natural history and literature, such as Karl Kroeber's *Ecological Literary Criticism* (1994), Lawrence Buell's *The Environmental Imagination* (1995), and Cheryll Glotfelty and Harold Fromm's *The Ecocriticism Reader* (1996). A healthy conversation has begun across disciplinary boundaries, and we can expect some fresh storytelling on themes of literary ecology.

The ideas and questions of literary ecology will provide a base for the inquiries of this book. Perhaps the humanities and the biological sciences can be persuaded here to speak and to listen to one another with creative results for both.

Systems

Since the first universities were founded in the twelfth century, knowledge has been organized into "disciplines." These strange categories are somewhat like farmer's fields: places where only one crop is supposed to grow, surrounded by defensible boundaries within which proprietors (professors) can defend their properties and remove all weeds. Specialization of knowledge has become particularly intense in the twentieth century, with new departments and disciplines proliferating as new knowledge is reputedly increasing. I suspect that much of this growth is more political than epistemological, since disciplines are the means by which academic people earn respect, tenure, salary, and status, and they provide the administrative structure to manage the research grants faculty have won. Disciplines are the units of organization for universities, but they are not necessarily the natural divisions of knowledge into its component parts.

As specialized knowledge has become more sophisticated and arcane, it has itself begun to undermine specialization by discovering new systemic relationships that tend to blur disciplinary boundaries. Already, late in the last century, the new science of ecology was investigating relationships among the many parts of biological systems, and asserting that the study of process and relationships was as important as the study of entities in isolation. Then physicists like Werner Heisenberg, early in this century, confirmed that observers are participants in every process that they observe, raising further doubts about the myth of scientific objectivity and detachment. Other hard-headed needs, such as the necessity for figuring out how to route millions of telephone calls or to keep track of enormous industrial inventories, led to the development of complex modeling techniques, and to the modern belief that creating models of complex systems is itself a path toward knowledge.

The rapid rise of computer technology has further accelerated the growth of systemic thinking. Intricate calculations and measurements that were once beyond human capability have become commonplace. The ability to simulate turbulent systems such as weather patterns and stream flows has grown along with chaos mathematics, fractal geometry, and studies in complex dynamic systems. These developments have changed the intellectual climate, disposing many thinkers to view their areas of interest from new perspectives, and to grant the possibility that multiple levels of interpretation may be simultaneously possible.

Interdisciplinary studies have thus become both respectable and necessary in modern intellectual life. Even though specialized disciplines become ever more sophisticated, they are increasingly contained only by permeable boundaries, not by rigid barriers. Like skin and cell walls, disciplinary borders breathe and take nourishment from the bodies of knowledge surrounding them. This book will honor that process, drawing from scientific, literary, philosophical, and social studies as they bear upon the topics before us. One fundamental premise of this work is that only a complex perspective can hope to comprehend the dynamics of life on Earth. I will try in the chapters ahead to explain these dynamics, and to provide models of how they might work.

Comedy and Play

And what are the topics before us? Sinus Block, my severe grandfather, might say that comedy and play are trivial subjects, unworthy of the attention of mature adults. That seems to have been the majority opinion in Western culture for many centuries. There are good reasons for reconsidering that opinion now. Comic literature is a human universal, occurring in every known culture and period. I also hope to show that, as a pattern of behavior and response to stimulus, comedy is a mode of action common to many animal species, and apparently is rooted deeply in evolutionary history. It is a way of life that seeks congruence with whatever dynamics are at work in a given time or place. When disruptions or threats to living processes occur, the comic way is to restore normalcy if possible. In better times, the comic search is for joy.

Play is the enactment of the comic spirit. Just as ritual puts myth into visible form, so play is comedy in action. Play is a universal human language that can cross cultural and linguistic boundaries. It is a sign of normalcy and health in many young animals, and several species, including our own, are capable of lifelong play. Play promotes equality among playmates, and accommodates novelty and spontaneity in their relationships. Genuine play is not goal-oriented behavior, but it appears to provide a necessary foundation for successful living, and perhaps for the creation of art, music, and literature.

Exactly how comedy and play do all of this is difficult to say. Precise definitions of either comedy or play are hard to find, and when found, prove inadequate to their purpose. Both are extremely complex patterns of thought and behavior, and can generally be described only by reference to the particular contexts in which they occur. That is, comedy and play are different according to who is doing them, where and when they are being done, and what other forces are interacting at the moment. No abstract definitions will cover all those bases. Good advice for people who want to think about comedy and play is to be prepared for novelty and surprise.

The next two chapters will describe the comic and tragic traditions in literature, and will try to see how these forms have influenced human values and affected human relationships with the natural world. Then a particular work, Shakespeare's *Hamlet*, will be examined for the mixture of comedy and tragedy it contains, and for the enigmas at the core of the work. Pastoral and picaresque literature show the variety of ways in which people have tried to figure out their relationships with natural settings, and these forms will occupy us for a chapter. By that time, I hope to be ready to consider the ethical implications of comedy and play, and to use a chapter for developing some fresh ethical ideas that fit with the comic way. At the end, we will be in the company of the highest comedy I know of, the spiritual poetry of Dante's *Commedia*. With Dante's help, we may find our way toward a high and cosmic play. The book will then conclude by toying with a play ethic.

Although serious people may think that comedy is silly, I believe that it holds truths that speak to the deepest parts of human nature. Comedy also moderates healthy relations among people, and between people and the Earth's natural processes. It connects us with other species through shared evolutionary history, and through present play that crosses species lines. Comedy is a contributor to survival, and a habit that promotes health.

2 * The Comic Way

The comic way is not always funny. Humor is sometimes a part of the comic experience (as it also is of tragic experience), but humor is not essential to the meaning of comedy. Comedy is more an attitude toward life and the self, and a strategy for dealing with problems and pain. A story from my youth may help to illustrate the nature of the comic way.

All their neighbors seem to take advantage of the caribou. Scores of insects and parasites have learned how to spend part of their life cycle in caribou guts and skin. Major predators such as wolves and bears depend upon caribou as a diet staple. Human hunters find them easy targets when they come close out of apparent curiosity. Although both male and female caribou grow large antlers, they are not known for ferocity in self-defense. Caribou security lies in their swiftness of flight, and in the safety of the herd.

Caribou migrations occur in the spring, when many thousands of animals may move together in search of the tundra lichens that are their basic food. As caribou luck would have it, this is also the time when the females are likely to give birth to calves. Females can be seen stepping out of the migrating herd to find a private spot for birthing, often on a slope near the migration path. Ordinarily, this works well enough, for a newborn caribou is able to keep up with the herd pace within ten minutes after birth. The new mother and her offspring usually rejoin the herd without a fuss, and the migration continues, one caribou stronger.

Other animals know about this odd caribou strategy, and often pay attention to it. My wife and I, for instance, were watching the migration through binoculars from a hillside in what is now Denali National Park, where I was a young park ranger in 1957. The migration that year included perhaps one hundred thousand caribou, and their passage over the tundra and braided gravel river bars took many days. We were new Alaskans, drinking in the marvels of abundant wildlife and great, free space. Another witness to the scene was a large grizzly bear, newly emerged from hibernation, and hungry.

A female caribou stepped aside from the migration and laboriously climbed a gentle slope for perhaps a hundred yards. She lay down on the tundra and began to give birth. The bear approached out of sight through the willows in a nearby creek bed, then charged when he was only a short distance from the cow's birthing place. The calf was seized just as it emerged from the mother, its spine broken by a quick jerk of the bear's neck. The mother leaped to her feet immediately in a posture of attack, and lowered her antlers to charge the bear. The bear was ready, threatening with teeth and claws as it stood over the bloody calf, outweighing the caribou by perhaps three hundred pounds.

Every impulse known to mammalian motherhood was evident in that caribou cow as she wrestled with her own emotions and with the choices available to her. She circled the scene, now lowering her head to attack, then backing off nervously at the futility of it. The bear kept her in sight, ready to respond to her moves, but proceeded to eat her calf before her eyes. Her anguish was evident in every move she made, alternately pacing, prancing, threatening, retreating, cowering, shivering, shaking her head in disbelief, staring. Within ten minutes the calf was mostly consumed, its mother a witness to its disappearance. The bear made a final lunge toward the cow, then turned and walked off. She turned, too, and slowly rejoined the migration.

Watching from a safe distance, our agitation seemed almost as great as that of the mother caribou. The distance between us and the scene of death was closed by our empathy. The basic emotions of tragedy, pity and fear, consumed us. We writhed and wept with the mother and her lost calf as if we were sharing their experience, which of course we were. Many years later, the details of that fifteen minutes on the tundra are as vivid to me as if they were happening in the present. We were spectators at a drama representing fundamental emotions common to all mammals, repeated endlessly whenever grief and loss occur because of the fragility of life and the power of death.

Yet what we saw was not a tragedy in the human sense of the term. The caribou mother did not bring her suffering upon herself by an act of will, as Medea did. She did not experience the polarization of good and evil, as Oedipus did. She did not discover a Hamlet-like rottenness in Denmark, or learn that she was born to set it right. Her impulse toward heroism was tempered by her clear assessment of the possibilities open to her. She saw and accepted her limitations, and was not compelled to transcend them. With all her grief and anger, with every hormone in her body raging, she remained a caribou, rejoining her kind on their path. As best she could in the circumstances, she returned to normal. Tragedy is a pattern that Western culture has developed over many centuries to deal with loss, grief, and death. It provides a framework that elevates suffering and makes metaphysical sense of misery. The tragic way also makes it hard to return to normal.

Not every catastrophe is a tragedy, and not everything comic is humorous. Both tragedy and comedy arise from experiences of misfortune, but they respond to pain in very different ways. The tragic way is to locate suffering according to a polarized idea of contrasts: good and evil, light and dark, God and the Devil, truth and falsehood, male and female, friend and enemy. Tragedy occurs when one makes a commitment to the positive end of the polar pair, then suffers from the corresponding negative end. Oedipus dedicates his life to moral purity, and suffers from moral pollution. King Lear bets everything on the loyalty and love of his children, and suffers their scorn and betrayal. The tragic mode of living requires that we perceive the world as a contest among warring camps, that we make choices among them, and that we bear full responsibility for the consequences of our choices. Tragedy occurs when we realize fully the painful consequences of choices we have made. That is why tragic dramas generally end with a funeral or its equivalent, to show that a sequence of willed events has led to its ultimate consequence.

The comic way, on the other hand, is the path of reconciliation. When the usual patterns of life are disrupted, the comic spirit strives for a return to normalcy. The comic vision is not polarized, but complex: comedy sees many aspects simultaneously, and seeks for a strategy that will resolve problems with a minimum of pain and confrontation. The comic way is not heroic or idealistic; rather, it is a strategy for survival.

The caribou mother experienced a catastrophe of the most compelling power, but her response was comic, not tragic. She recognized her limitations, saw and felt her loss, and rejoined the flow of caribou life.

The Biology of Comedy

Any human can feel empathy for the caribou mother because the emotions she was experiencing are universal among mammals. Comic literature takes such universals as its normal subject matter. Literary comedy appears wherever human culture exists. Comedy can be universal because it depends less upon particular ideologies or metaphysical systems than tragedy does. Rather, comedy grows from the biological circumstances of life. It is unconcerned with cultural systems of morality. Comedy literally has no use for morality, for moral insights play no significant role in the comic experience. Similarly, comedy normally avoids strong emotions. Passionate love, hate, or patriotism generally appear ridiculous in a comic context, for comedy tends to create a psychological mood that is incompatible with deep emotions. Great ideas and ideals fare no better at the hands of comedy, which ordinarily treats them as if they were insignificant. When noble idealism does appear in comedy, its vehicle is commonly a Tartuffe (as in Molière's *Tartuffe: or The Impostor*) or a Malvolio (as in Shakespeare's *Twelfth Night*), whose nobility turns out to be merely a sham to conceal selfish or ignoble motives. The comic view demonstrates that people behave irrationally, committing follies that reveal their essential ignorance and ridiculousness in relation to civilized systems of ethical and social behavior. Aristotle believed that comedy imitates the actions of people who are inferior to the social norm, just as tragedy imitates the actions of superior people.

Comedy demonstrates that humans are durable, although they may be weak, stupid, and undignified. As the tragic hero suffers or dies for ideals, the comic hero survives without them. At the end of his tale he manages to marry his girl, evade his enemies, slip by the oppressive authorities, avoid drastic punishment, and stay alive. His victories are all small, but he lives in a world where only small victories are possible. His career demonstrates that weakness is a normal condition that humans must live with. Comedy is careless of goodness, truth, beauty, heroism, and all such abstract values people often claim to live by. Its main concern is to affirm the human capacity for survival and to celebrate the continuity of life itself, despite all moralities. Comedy is a celebration, a ritual renewal of biological welfare as it persists in spite of any reasons there may be for feeling metaphysical despair.

The Greek demigod Comus, whose name was the likely origin of the word comedy, was a god of fertility in a large but unpretentious sense. His concerns included the ordinary sexual fertility of plants, animals, and people, and also the general success of family and community life insofar as these depend upon biological processes. Comus was content to leave matters of great intellectual import to Apollo and gigantic passions to Dionysus while he busied himself with maintenance of the commonplace conditions that are friendly to life. Maintaining equilibrium among living things, and restoring it when it had been lost, were Comus's special talents, and they are shared by the many comic characters who follow the god's example.

The comic way is not a path toward power. Apollo and Dionysus, the gods of tragedy, represent intellectual, emotional, political, and economic power, and their creations demonstrate how power works to create glory and misery in human affairs. The comic creations of Comus express the ways of those who are not in power. The ways of women have often been comic ways, strategic and clever rather than forceful and invasive. The poor and the enslaved know comic techniques of evasive action and misdirection to save their skins and get what they need for survival. Power is the ability to impose one's will upon others; comedy is the ability to meet one's needs with wit and imagination.

Literary comedy depicts the loss of equilibrium and its recovery. Wherever the normal processes of life are obstructed unnecessarily, the comic way seeks to return to normal. Comedy was a well-established literary form in the fifth century B.C., when the playwright Aristophanes began to use it. In his play *Lysistrata*, Athens and Sparta are at war, and all able-bodied men are off fighting for their country. An Athenian woman, Lysistrata, decides to do something to remedy the unfortunate situation that keeps husbands from their wives' beds and puts sons in danger. She gathers the Athenian women and persuades them to join her in a sex strike to end the war. The women agree to make themselves as sexually alluring as possible to their men, but to give them no satisfaction. Aristophanes' play then spins its comic story of seduction and frustration, until at last the generals from both sides are led by their erect penises to the peace table where they end the war. Husbands return to their wives' beds, and young men are safe once more at home. This is the basic pattern of comic action.

Comedy is not a heroic undertaking, but a strategic one. No great truths are unveiled in the process, and no triumph over evil is won. Wit and cleverness are put in the service of maintaining the essential conditions for life, especially sex and safety. The ending is commonly a wedding or a reconciliation, where opposing forces are once more at peace with one another.

The best thing about comedy is that it is a *way* of perceiving the world and responding to it; a *way* of feeling that is free of sentiment; a *way* of thinking according to wholes made up of clearly recognized parts; and a *way* of acting according to the needs of the context and the tenor of the time. Comedy is a process that proceeds according to its own principles, although it sometimes appears to be unprincipled. In modern terms, comedy is systemic.

Infinite Play

A helpful perspective on the comic way is provided by James P. Carse in his pithy little book, *Finite and Infinite Games*.[1] As Carse puts it, "A finite game is played for the purpose of winning, an infinite game for the purpose of continuing the play."[2] Finite games, in other words, are those played for the purpose of ending the game with a victory or a defeat. These are contests, and are familiar to us in the form of wars, most sporting events, politics as usual, business dealings, and the ordinary competitiveness of daily life. Finite games are characterized by having clear goals, rules, and sometimes a referee or other authority (like the courts) to make sure that they are played correctly. We will consider finite games more thoroughly in the next chapter.

In an infinite game, "the only purpose of the game is to prevent it from coming to an end, and to keep everyone in play."[3] Infinite play is a manifestation of the comic way. It can be found in the play of children and of animals, in enduring love, in evolution and natural selection, in symbiosis and cooperations of all kinds, and in all those forms of behavior that are so satisfying that we want them to go on and on. My favorite working definition of play is that it is spontaneous behavior whose only purpose is to please its participants and keep them playing. When goals or objectives appear, or when rules become rigid, play disappears.

The most endearing thing about play is its uselessness. Play exists for its own sake, and seeks no goals or objectives beyond itself. Most games are not playful, for wherever there are prizes, rules, or judges, playfulness disappears and the spirit of warfare, or at least of contest, presides. There is no way to win while playing catch with your kid, and people on surfboards have no real destinations. The only genuine reason for playing is to continue playing.

During play, all players are equal. If there are inequities of power, weight, agility, or age, they must be offset by handicapping the stronger players. Squirrel monkeys who wrestle unequally on the ground because one outweighs the other can establish equity by hanging from branches and wrestling in midair. Adults of all species find ways to play on equal terms with their offspring, and professional athletes play by simpler rules when they enter sandlot games. There are no playful tyrants, and no tyrannical players.

Boundaries of all kinds are crossed during play. A stranger with an unknown language and culture will know how to respond if you smile and toss him a ball. Play is one of the rare human languages that can cross all lines of culture, race, gender, status, or species. When your dog makes a mock pounce at you, it is clear that playtime is at hand. Most species have such clear behavioral signals to express invitations to play, and they use them with their own kind or with any other species that seems willing to play.

Satisfying sexual relationships include a strong element of play. Sexuality that is only passionate, with no play included, is in danger of becoming possessive or manipulative. Like other kinds of play, sexual play calls for innovation, novelty, equity between partners, and willingness to take a few risks just to see what the results may be.

Most play involves risks of some kind. Playful curiosity leads us to stick our noses where they've never been before, or to test just how far we can crawl out on that limb before it breaks. Among humans and other species, play behavior is a frequent cause of injury or death. For play to have been retained as a widespread pattern in many forms of life through millions of years of evolutionary history, the rewards must have been worth the costs.

Art is one of the rewards for our species. We play music, attend theatrical plays, and play with color, sound, words, movement, and form in a thousand artful ways. When art involves the creation of an imaginary reality, even a grim reality like literary tragedy, it is a playful experience. The play of great art calls for high skills and imagination, and reminds us that the world itself can be our gigantic playground.

Art, like play, sometimes takes risks that threaten the tidiness that civilization values so highly. Art and play are sources of new experience and they encourage change, so they worry people who like things to stay put and be obedient. They are not the kinds of activities that fit into neat categories, and they are both full of surprises.

Comic Evolution

Humans did not invent comedy or play. We are, rather, the comic and playful beneficiaries of millions of years of evolutionary history. There is some disagreement about how far back on the phylogenetic scale playful behavior appears in animals, but the consensus opinion seems to be that play enters the evolutionary story in the company of the birds and mammals, in the Jurassic era of some 150 to 200 million years ago, long before the earliest humanoid creatures.

Robert Fagen has done more than anyone to provide insight and understanding about animal play. His comprehensive book, *Animal Play Behavior*,[4] provides detailed information about every animal species that is known to include play in its normal behavior. Fagen believes that play is for the phylogenetically privileged: "Play is a minority phenomenon in nature. The evolution of play precisely mirrors the evolution of the brain. Play and a highly developed cerebral cortex go together."[5] The brain gives animals an opportunity to expand their perceptual and behavioral repertoires, and to venture into new and unexpected levels of experience. Play may be one of the ways the newly emerged brain developed in order to accommodate novelty and to explore the unknown.

That complex brain shared by birds and mammals evolved in response to wilderness ecosystems where the brains were not in control of things, but were at their best when responding appropriately to some new feature or challenge. Competition and warfare sometimes seem to be the most common uses of the brain in relating to its surrounding world, but we are also learning that brains are superb at the arts of cooperation. Robert Axelrod's landmark study, *The Evolution of Cooperation*,[6] describes a series of computer simulations in which the basic principles of cooperative behavior are discovered as they apply to many kinds of complex systems such as economies, weather patterns, immune systems, stock markets, and scores of other human and nonhuman systems.

Surprisingly, Axelrod showed that "cooperation can get started by even a small cluster of individuals who are prepared to reciprocate cooperation, even in a world where no one else will cooperate."[7] And it doesn't take high ideals or noble intentions to achieve cooperation:

> The individuals do not have to be rational: the evolutionary process allows the successful strategies to thrive, even if the players do not know why or how. Nor do the players have to exchange messages or commitments: they do not need words, because their deeds speak for them. Likewise, there is no need to assume trust between players: the use of reciprocity can be enough to make defection unproductive. Altruism is not needed: successful strategies can elicit cooperation even from an egoist. Finally, no central authority is needed: cooperation based on reciprocity can be self-policing.[8]

The principles of cooperation strongly resemble the basic conditions of play and the comic way. They require no cultural or ideological enforcement, for they appear to be built into the evolutionary structure of life at its smallest levels: "if bacteria can play games, so can people and nations."[9] The game that life is playing is an infinite game, played in order to keep the game alive.

Evolution is the temporal order of the game of life, and natural selection is its decision-making process. Evolution proceeds as an unscrupulous, opportunistic comedy, the object of which appears to be the proliferation and preservation of as many life forms as possible. Successful participants in it are those who live and reproduce even when times are hard or dangerous, not those who are best able to destroy enemies or competitors. Its ground rules for participants, including people, are those that also govern literary comedy: Organisms must adapt themselves to their circumstances in every possible way, must studiously avoid all-or-nothing choices, must seek alternatives to death, must accept and revel in maximum diversity, must accommodate themselves to the accidental limitations of birth and environment, and must prefer cooperation to competition, yet compete successfully when necessary. Comic action, in literature or in natural history, follows naturally from these principles.

As evolution organizes time, so ecology reflects spatial organization, describing the complex dynamics that connect the many millions of organisms alive at any given time on this planet. Structural principles of ecology also show the comic way at work. Each species in an ecosystem is affected by the actions and events of other species, so that the whole is an ever-changing process that never ends or holds still. Energy and nutrients flow through the ecosystem, causing a constant rearrangement of the major elements, revising and recombining parts of the system in never-ending variety. As each niche in an ecosystem is developed, new opportunities and possibilities are created for other niches, assuring that novelty and surprise are ever present. Natural ecosystems are excellent places to observe infinite play, where endless spontaneity stirs the pot in a process that exists only to keep itself playing.

The comic way is to be found in evolutionary history, in the processes of ecology, and in comic literature, which may represent the closest we have come to describing humans as adaptive animals. Comedy illustrates that survival depends upon our ability to change ourselves rather than our environment, and upon our ability to accept limitations rather than to curse fate for limiting us. We can learn from a grieving mother caribou how to go on with life after terrible losses. Comedy is a strategy for living that contains ecological wisdom, and it may be one of our best guides as we try to retain a place for ourselves among the other animals that live according to the comic way.

3 * *Tragedy and Related Disasters*

Sinus Block, my unhappy grandfather, lived a sad life but not a tragic one. His world was grim, from the poverty of his youth to the mortuary business that made him wealthy. His German-Baptist fundamentalism kept him always mindful of the sinfulness of life, but it also gave him a simple but clear moral stance that sharply distinguished between good and evil. A similar polarization governed his political life, where patriots inhabited heaven, and hell was for all atheists, socialists, Bolsheviks, unionists, and other purveyors of perverted doctrines. Sinus was known as a great patron of patriotic festivals, especially Decoration Day (now Memorial Day, it was in Sinus's time an occasion for visiting cemeteries, his place of business) and the Fourth of July. Sinus always invested in bunting to decorate the town, and usually led the parade, especially after he bought the first motorized hearse in town. The flag was also, of course, good protective coloring for a German immigrant during the anti-German sentiments of World War I. His ideologies were conveniently good for his image, and for his business. His funeral-and-furniture business, and his substantial land holdings, established Sinus as a man of power and privilege.

Even without knowing more about Sinus than, perhaps, those parts of him that survive in me as genetic heritage, it is possible to infer some things about his values and beliefs because they represent a familiar pattern in European and American culture. Goal-oriented behavior, a need for power and control, a highly polarized scheme for judging good and evil or friends and enemies, and a sense of self that affirms personal dignity and requires deference from others: these are traits easily found in modern Western cultures of the past few centuries. They rest, I believe, upon even deeper origins in the Greek and Hebrew roots of modern culture, and in the traditions of literary tragedy.

Tragic literature is unusually inclusive of the values of the civilizations that produced it. No other literary form incorporates metaphysical, moral, social, and emotional attitudes in a matrix as tightly unified as tragedy's. None has more clearly expressed human ideals or measured their implications. Tragic literature is a mirror with impeccably sharp resolution and high selectivity. Its image of humanity is a genuine reflection of our deepest and most significant qualities, but not of all of them. Like other mirrors, tragedy discriminates among available sources of imagery, selectively emphasizing those qualities it was created to display. Tragic writers have consistently chosen to affirm those values that regard the personal self as the pinnacle of all worth, and that regard the world as humanity's personal property.

Tragedy is not synonymous with catastrophe. Newspaper headlines notwithstanding, it is not a tragedy when train wrecks, floods, or earthquakes kill thousands or when an innocent child is run down by an automobile. Such accidents cause pain and death to many who do not deserve to suffer, but they are not tragic. Genuine tragic suffering is a consequence of deliberate choice. Tragic figures bring on their own suffering, for they have taken a course of action that must inevitably lead to their doom, even though they may not have been aware at an early stage of the consequences of their choice. They become tragic because they accept responsibility for their actions and face their pain with the full knowledge that they have brought it on themselves. Their courage is admired even while they are pitied for their suffering. Tragedy, unlike catastrophe, is comforting and flattering. It presents the world as an ordered place where some kind of justice or morality rules. The universe is shown to care enough about people to punish them when they go astray, rather like a stern but compassionate judge. And people appear as a worthy object of love, for they have the capacity to grow and to learn, even to the point of transcending many of their own weaknesses and limitations. Tragic people are ennobled by their struggles, and humanity is ennobled by witnessing their ordeals.

Tragedy is a cultural invention, not a product of evolutionary history. The tragic view of life is a unique feature of Western civilization with no true counterpart in primitive or Oriental cultures. It was developed by the Greeks and later modified within the context of the Judeo-Christian tradition. Individual elements of the tragic view of life are present in many cultures, but the peculiar conglomeration of ideas and beliefs that constitutes literary tragedy is a distinctive feature of the West. Further, literary tragedy and environmental exploitation in Western culture share many of the same philosophical presuppositions. Neither tragedy nor environmental crisis could have developed as they have without the interweaving of a few basic ideas that have attained in the Western tradition an importance far greater than they carry in other cultures.

Three such ideas will illustrate the point: the assumption that nature exists for the benefit of humanity, the belief that human morality transcends natural limitations, and humanism's insistence upon the supreme importance of the individual personality. All are characteristic beliefs that appear implicitly and explicitly in tragic literature. As these beliefs have gradually eroded or been rejected, tragedy has lost much of its power.

Humanity's Very Own Environment

Hebraic and Greek cultures have asserted from their beginnings that nature exists for the benefit of humanity. In the Genesis account of creation, plants and animals are created to be useful to Adam, and the Garden of Eden is supplied as a fit environment to meet human needs. Adam receives "dominion over the fish of the sea, and over the fowl of the air, and over the cattle, and over all the earth, and over every creeping thing that creepeth upon the earth." Whether "dominion" is to be interpreted to mean responsible stewardship or wanton exploitation is an old debate among theologians, but at least exploitation is not clearly ruled out. Adam and his progeny have felt themselves licensed to use their dominion to their own advantage, for it is obvious that people are very important and creeping things aren't.

The Greeks saw nature more as a challenge to human ingenuity than as a god-given source of sustenance, but the superior status of people over nature was never doubted. The choral ode from Sophocles' *Antigone* elaborates the theme of human supremacy, emphasizing human technological superiority over nature and the miracle of human mentality:

Many the wonders but nothing walks stranger than man.
This thing crosses the sea in winter's storm,
making his path through the roaring waves.

And she, the greatest of gods, the earth—
ageless she is, and unwearied—he wears her away
as the ploughs go up and down from year to year
and his mules turn up the soil.

Gay nations of birds he snares and leads,
wild beast tribes and the salty brood of the sea,
with the twisted mesh of his nets, this clever man.
He controls with craft the beasts of the open air,
walkers on hills. The horse with his shaggy mane
he holds and harnesses, yoked about the neck
and the strong bull of the mountain.

Language, and thought like the wind
and the feelings that make the town
he has taught himself, and shelter against the cold,
refuge from rain. He can always help himself.
He faces no future helpless. There's only death
that he cannot find escape from. He has contrived
refuge from illnesses once beyond all cure.

Clever beyond all dreams
the inventive craft that he has
which may drive him one time or another to well or ill.
When he honors the laws of the land and the gods' sworn right
High indeed is his city; but stateless the man
who dares to dwell with dishonor.[1]

Although the Earth is "the greatest of gods" rather than a garden created for human use, people are greater still by virtue of their inventiveness and power. It is no accident that a rhapsody extolling human conquests over nature appears at a crucial point in Greek tragic drama, for the human elevation above natural environments is an essential tragic assertion. Humanity is here being praised at the expense of nature, and only humanity is of interest to the poet. Although the land is worn away by human plows and the nations of birds presumably lose their gaiety once they are snared, there is no shame but only praise for the clever people who can inflict this damage for their own benefit. Human dignity is assumed to be independent of and superior to nature, although the conquest of nature is a necessary precondition for its realization. Sophocles has here made explicit the human superiority over nature that is an essential feature of the tragic view of life. It is not that the struggle to control nature is itself tragic, for people are said to master their biological problems with relative ease. The real difficulties are social and metaphysical: How to live with the law and what to do about death, and to meet both problems with something called honor.

Honor and dignity, from either the Greek or the Hebrew perspective, depend upon spiritual states that transcend nature. In both cultures ethical laws derived from metaphysical principles define the proper activities of people. For the Hebrews, obedience to divine law and devotion to God are supernatural allegiances that determine human excellence. For the Greeks, social order and intellectual integrity are the highest values. Both assume human elevation above the processes of nature.

Unnatural Morality

Corollary to the belief in human supremacy is the assumption of a metaphysical moral order that also transcends nature. Greek and Hebrew sources are again unanimous in this belief, although they vary in its application. Fate, destiny, the will of God or gods, justice, salvation, honor, are just a few of the terms used to identify the nature of universal order. In modern attempts at tragedy, order is more likely to be described in social terms. All these concepts share the supposition that the welfare of humanity depends upon our ability to live up to a preexisting standard of virtuous behavior, and that this standard is essentially supranatural, the product of spiritual, intellectual, or social powers not governed by the processes of nature. Among the Greeks, violation of the moral order leads to tragedy;

the Hebrews and Christians regarded such violations as sins leading to damnation.

Only humans can experience tragedy or damnation since the moral order specifically governs human affairs and does not apply to the rest of creation. Dogs may mate with their mothers without encountering the moral problems of Oedipus, lions may walk into traps without pondering the destiny that moved them to do so, and the many nearly extinct species of plants and animals are not questioners of divine justice as the biblical Job was when he saw disasters on every hand. Of all the millions of species of plants and animals, tragedy is for humans alone.

Tragedy is more concerned with moral pollution, an exclusively human phenomenon, than with the biologically universal experiences of disaster and pain. Only humans can sin by departing from the moral order, and humans alone can purify themselves by reestablishing their harmony with that order. "Thy people which thou broughtest out of the land of Egypt have corrupted themselves," says the Lord as he delivers the tables of the law into Moses' hands.[2] Better law is the typical Hebrew prescription for the disease of sin. The Ten Commandments undertake to purify the people by a more perfect regulation of their social behavior and by establishing ritual observances that will remind them of their dependence upon divine power. As prophets interpreted moral law for the Hebrews, so tragic dramatists interpreted it for the Greeks. Tragedy is a ritual purification, in Aristotle's term a catharsis, that immerses us in moral corruption in order to free us from it. We see in the tragic hero the consequences of overstepping the boundaries of moral law; in the process, the existence and validity of the law itself are demonstrated.

The Greeks were quite as insistent as the Hebrews that moral law originated above and beyond the sphere of natural existence. Plato's analogy of the cave in *The Republic* is intended to demonstrate that human perceptions are generally false, and that the source of both morality and truth is far removed from mundane experience. Platonic ideas of goodness, truth, and beauty are independent of experience and unalterable by human actions. All humans can do is to discover their existence and contemplate their meaning, which is what Plato recommends as the proper activity of philosophers. Tragic heroes encounter these absolutes when the actions of their lives run contrary to moral law, and they suffer accordingly.

The Tragic Ego

Although belief in human superiority over nature and in the existence of absolute moral law were common to Greek and Hebrew cultures, it was only the Greeks who originated genuine tragedy. The unique humanism of the Greeks placed special emphasis on the individual human personality. While the Hebrews were concerned with the social problems of the chosen people, the Greeks tended to focus upon the psychological problems of the chosen individual. The exceptional personality is always at the heart of Greek tragedy, and of the tragic tradition that flows from it.

The tragic hero (or, rarely, heroine) is an isolated man bearing on his private shoulders the moral burdens of all humanity. He takes himself very seriously, and acts upon the assumption that his personal fate is a matter of great consequence to the world in general. Aristotle's "high-minded" man is one who is conscious of his superior power and intellect, generous with his wealth, and confident of his importance. His pride is the proper mean between groveling humility and selfish vanity. Tragic heroes share these qualities but suffer from some flaw that brings about their destruction in a morally instructive way without decreasing our admiration for them. The tragic hero is a remarkable individual deserving of simultaneous admiration and pity. The extraordinary value attached by the Greeks to such individual personalities is one of their more influential contributions to the Western tradition. Tragedy is unthinkable without it.

The unique individual is the focal point of all significance in tragic literature. The tragic hero may be a symbolic person like a king in classical tragedy, or a typical member of a social group or a psychological type in realistic modern tragedy, but it is his unique personality that is the center of tragic action. He must be highly individualized so that the spectator may experience intense empathy and share his suffering even while recognizing that the hero is in many respects different from the spectator. If he is too generalized, then the focus will shift from character to idea and the result is a problem drama rather than a tragedy. If he is too clearly symbolic of a larger group or of a personality type, the result is an allegory or melodrama. The essential tragic character is one whose uniqueness is not diminished by the fact that he is also a representative of humanity. The Greek tragic heroes who embody this delicate balance—such as Achilles, Oedipus, and Orestes—are among the most admired symbolic characters of the Western cultural tradition.

It is worthwhile to distinguish between tragic heroes and cultural heroes of the type found in biblical literature and in other ancient mythologies. Culture heroes represent their people and reinforce the will of the gods, and they stand as moral exemplars. Jacob, Joseph, Moses, and the entire array of Old Testament heroes act for their people as a whole. Their personalities are submerged in the larger process of divine destiny in which they merely play their part. They see themselves as instruments in the hands of God performing divinely ordained tasks. Their actions follow what appears to be a universal pattern for culture heroes: departure, initiation, and return bearing a new message of truth for the good of humanity. This is not the pattern of the tragic hero. He does not undertake a quest for a new truth to benefit humanity, but acts in response to personal challenges.

Nor is the tragic hero a leader of his nation or culture in the sense that his actions provide a model for others to follow. Rama, the culture hero of the ancient Hindu epic, the *Ramayana*, is clearly an exemplar of the best virtues of his culture, useful for instructing youthful aspirants in the proper methods of heroism and selflessness. The imitation of Rama has occupied Hindus for centuries, much as the imitation of Christ has governed religious and ethical instruction in Christian cultures. But no one would found an educational tradition upon the imitation of such tragic characters as Achilles, Oedipus, Antigone, Hamlet, or King Lear, partly because they are sinners, but also because their characters are unique and inimitable.

Greek tragedy demonstrates that unique human individuals are capable of experiences that go beyond the capacity of humanity in general; the tragic hero exists as proof of that thesis. Neither the laws of nature nor human laws are absolute boundaries to the tragic hero, but are rather challenges that he must test by attempting to transcend them. The suffering that accompanies his struggle or results from it is merely a price that must be paid for his momentary freedom from the restraints accepted by all other creatures.

In his penetrating analysis of Homer's Achilles, classical scholar Cedric Whitman articulated the proposition that all great tragedy demonstrates: "The highest heroes are . . . men of clarity and purity, who will a good impossible in the world, and eventually achieve it, through suffering, in their own spiritual terms."[3] This aspiration to accomplish the impossible constitutes the uniqueness of the tragic hero and makes him both admirable and terrible. Whitman identifies Homer's Achilles as the first such hero in literature, but adds that "the baffling vision of self-destruction with eternal glory was native to Greek air, and Homer was the first to frame it in the symbols of poetry and canonize it for the succeeding ages of the Hellenic, and especially the Athenian, mind."[4] The Athenian mind built tragic drama on this unprecedented combination of transcendence and annihilation and set a standard that people and authors have since tried to match.

Into the foundations of Western culture was built the idea that personal greatness is achieved at the cost of great destruction. The power of Greek tragedy has etched that idea deeply into the Western mind. Although few may have the personal attributes of an Achilles, it is no great trouble to translate the tragic assumptions into more modest terms in order to enjoy a smaller share. Sinus Block may have figured that moderate greatness may be achieved at the cost of moderate destruction. And it only requires a small adjustment of one's blinders to overlook the fact that the tragic hero destroys mostly himself, although there is some peripheral destruction of others (Troy is sacked, and the kingdoms of Oedipus, Hamlet, and Lear are left in disorder). The true imitation of tragic heroes is difficult, but it is relatively easy to absorb their lesson that any cost is justified for the fulfillment of the unique personality.

Tragic heroes do not generally contend against their natural environments, nor are they exploiters of nature. When Achilles battles the River Xanthos or when Lear challenges the thunderstorm, their real enemies are themselves; the elements of nature are merely used by the poets to represent the inner struggles within the character of the hero. Tragedy is ultimately metaphysical, and it is always evident that biological problems of survival and welfare are of small concern. Tragedy is an art form concerned with moral order and the fulfillment of the individual personality, not with the conquest of nature.

Tragic art, together with the humanistic and theological ideologies upon which it rests, describes a world in which the processes of nature are relatively unimportant and always subservient to human interests. Nobility, honor, dignity, and spiritual purification depend upon supranatural forces in the tragic view, not upon conciliation with nature. The tragic view of life is proud to be unnatural.

The Decline of Tragedy

Over the past two or three centuries, tragedy has gradually died as an art form. Joseph Wood Krutch, the late American literary critic with a naturalist's eye, lamented the passing of this great tradition but noted that its demise was inevitable once the supporting ideology had lost its grip upon the Western mind. Krutch argued that the tragic view of life rests upon a logical error made early in the development of Western thought: "The Tragic Fallacy depends ultimately upon the assumption which man so readily makes that something outside his own being, some 'spirit not himself'—be it God, Nature, or that still vaguer thing called a Moral Order—joins him in the emphasis which he places upon this or that and confirms him in his feeling that his passions and his opinions are important."[5] Krutch notes that the intellectual history of recent centuries has presented evidence that seems almost unanimously to contradict these assumptions of tragic literature.

The decline of tragic values has proceeded gradually but continuously since the Renaissance. Every major attempt at tragedy since the Elizabethans has revealed a progressive weakening or rejection of the ideological prerequisites to a tragic view of human experience. The three tragic assumptions examined here—the existence of a transcendent moral order, the assumption of human supremacy over nature, and the importance of the unique human individual—have suffered both reasoned contradiction from science and philosophy and the loss of their former power to excite the imagination.

The Naturalization of Morality

William Shakespeare, writing in the late sixteenth century, could not permit his characters to assert human superiority with anything like the confidence of Sophocles in the fifth century B.C. Shakespeare's Hamlet, musing over the human condition, repeats many of the terms of the choral ode from *Antigone*, but with irony, not as an assertion of obvious truth:

> What a piece of work is a man! How noble in reason!
> How infinite in faculty! In form and moving how
> express and admirable! In action how like an angel!

In apprehension how like a god! The beauty of the world!
The paragon of animals!

(Hamlet, act 2, scene 2)

Hamlet is by no means certain that man is the paragon of animals. He is mouthing the humanist platitudes popular among Renaissance writers and epitomized by the fifteenth-century Italian humanist Pico della Mirandola in his "Oration on the Dignity of Man" (1486). The context of Hamlet's homily fails to confirm such platitudes. The humanist credo Hamlet has learned in school is no longer adequate to explain his experience. It is one possible view but not the only reasonable one, as it was for Sophocles. Similarly, Hamlet and the Elizabethan tragic heroes are uncertain about the existence of a moral order in the universe. "To be or not to be" is a question to be answered according to one's belief or disbelief in a spiritual and moral order that judges the actions of life and punishes or rewards them after death. Hamlet rejects suicide because he is uncertain whether it will make a difference to his soul, not because he is sure that it will.

Both moral order and human supremacy are questionable possibilities to Hamlet and to Shakespeare's contemporaries, but the importance of the unique individual is still an unquestionable truth. Hamlet knows that he, personally, was born to set right what is rotten in Denmark, and he sees throughout the play that his private decisions are all-important. His remarkable personality, compounded of an unusually keen intellect together with his emotional problems as "passion's slave," makes Hamlet an object of mystery to the other characters in the play and to the audiences who have studied him for four centuries. The center of the play is the personality of Hamlet. Even though moral order and human supremacy are doubtful, the importance of individual character remains a certainty. (Hamlet will be examined more closely in the next chapter.)

Morality as Social Behavior

The assumptions of nineteenth-century realistic tragedy reveal a further decay of tragic values. By the time of Henrik Ibsen, the nineteenth-century founder of the realistic theater, the belief in a transcendent moral order had all but disappeared. In its place are the secular orders and disorders of social law and custom. Ibsen's master builder seeks to be a hero by constructing homes for people rather than churches for God. He lives in a world that is neither just nor natural but is instead dominated by outworn social conventions, an exploitative industrial economy, and much personal pettiness. Human beings are shown to suffer or to prosper according to the nature of their relationships with one another and with contemporary society. They are not superior to nature, nor are they judged by the gods. If anything, Ibsen's characters, like many in realistic tragedy, seem to be inferior to the symbols of nature with which they are juxtaposed. In addition to Ibsen's wild duck, O'Neill's hairy ape and Chekhov's cherry orchard come to mind.

Although morality is reduced to social questions and human superiority to nature is ignored or denied, the primacy of character remains a sufficient foundation for whatever success realistic tragedy can claim. In *The Master Builder*, Ibsen's tragic character, Solness, explains and justifies his life in terms that would apply equally well to Greek or Elizabethan tragic heroes: "There are certain special, chosen people who have a gift and power and capacity to *wish* something, *desire* something, *will* something—so insistently and so—so inevitably—that at last it has to be theirs."[6] The remarkable character is crucial to realistic tragedy, for it is all that remains of the classical prerequisites for a tragic view of life.

The development of existential tragedy advances the suppositions of realism and the decline of tragedy one step further. Friedrich Nietzsche's *Uebermensch* and his successors are proud to deny metaphysical morality and to proclaim their kinship with the animals as they struggle to transcend traditional concepts of good and evil, but they never deny their own uniqueness. Ivan Karamazov, a central character in Dostoyevsky's novel *The Brothers Karamazov*, rejects the moral order with his argument that "everything is permitted" in a world where God and immortality have ceased to exist, yet he affirms his own uniqueness by his tragic acceptance of the moral responsibility that God no longer bears. The theme persists in existentialist literature and philosophy as humans assume the burdens that were formerly divine, with the result that the tragic assumption of human uniqueness is considerably magnified, while moral absolutes and superiority to nature have all but disappeared from tragic consciousness.

Deflation of the Tragic Ego

The twentieth century has rejected the last essential tenet of tragic belief, the potential transcendence of the individual personality. Modern tragicomedy, the theater of the absurd, and the *nouveau roman* constitute the first full-scale abandonment of the tragic view of life since its emergence in ancient Greece. Absurd characters are not allegorical everymen or tragic heroes in the classical sense, but merely commonplace human beings facing ordinary circumstances. Personality will neither save nor damn them, but is itself subordinate to their predicaments. Personality is thus less important than events, diminishing the possibility of conceiving a tragic hero.

The decline of tragedy coincides with major changes in attitudes toward the natural world over the past four centuries. Tragedy has depended upon philosophical ideas of the relationship between humanity and nature, both as a metaphysical foundation for a tragic view of experience and for metaphorical imagery used to express character and action. The twentieth century French novelist Alain Robbe-Grillet points out that our inherited conceptions of nature are "clogged with an anthropomorphic vocabulary" that has long since ceased to be expressive of our beliefs and feelings.[7] He argues therefore that literature must purge itself of the "pananthropic" notion that the entire universe has a special interest in the doings of humanity. Robbe-Grillet's rejection of the presuppositions of tragedy is sweeping and complete, and it grows directly from his denial of traditional views of nature: "There is, then, first a rejection of the analogical vocabulary [comparing humans to nature] and of traditional humanism, a rejection at the same time of the idea of tragedy, and of any other notion leading to the belief in a profound, and higher, nature of man or of things (and of the two together), a rejection, finally, of every pre-established order."[8] Robbe-Grillet's alternative is to describe creatures and things, humans included, without pretending that any necessary relationship exists among them. Without that pretense, tragedy is inconceivable.

Legacies of Tragedy

Tragedy has expired as an art form, but its influence persists in many parts of public and private life. It was there in the Protestant revolution of the sixteenth century with its strong new emphasis on the polarities of God and devil, good and evil. Puritans retained those polarities, but added the practical morality of the work ethic, with its goal-oriented passions and fear of all fun. Our inherited legal system is symbolized by a blind goddess holding the scales of justice, an image that was created in Greece at the same time as literary tragedy. It has come to stand for an adversarial legal system that turns whatever it touches into lies or truth, black or white.

The tragic taste for the remarkable individual also persists in the personality cults that collect around the figures of sports, television, and motion pictures (especially if they have managed to do something scandalous). Print and broadcast journalism feed these appetites, also providing tidily simplified accounts of complex topics that appear to make world affairs into matters of fairly plain choices. The partisanship and jingoism of modern politics also tends to reduce matters to simple all-or-nothing choices, and elections become battlegrounds between self-styled good guys and their supposed evil adversaries.

The tragic way of playing the game of life is the finite way, seeking a prize or a payoff that will bring status to the victor even if it does tend to end the game. That may be why a tragic view of life has remained so popular for such a long time. Like many fundamentalist beliefs, it rests upon the premise that for every question there is only one right answer, and for every possibility of behavioral action there is one correct choice. This often leads to the corollary belief that all competing answers and choices are wrong, evil, or both. It is a sharply polarized view of existence that appeals to many people, perhaps because it simplifies decision making, and provides certainties that often seem to be deeply rooted in dependable traditions. Comforting though that may be, its consequences are often disastrous in a world that is increasingly complex and systemic.

Tragedy or Pathos?

It is tempting to think of Western civilization as a collective image of the tragic hero facing ecological disaster just as tragic heroes have faced their personal crises. Our way of life has sought the good and brought evil upon ourselves as a consequence of our efforts, just as all tragic heroes have done. Our presumed conquest over nature has brought little genuine satisfaction, for with it has come the discovery that our very existence depends upon the complexity of natural systems that were destroyed in the process. The nobility of the tragic hero is not part of the modern character, and only his recklessness and irrationality remain. The story is now pathetic, not tragic.

Environmental disasters are not tragic, for they cannot be conceived as the moral error of an individual who has made a destructive choice. Oedipus caused the pollution of Thebes by his sinful murder and marriage, but who causes the pollution of New York? What was rotten in Denmark could be remedied by Hamlet, but who will take responsibility for what is rotten in Chicago? No hero will suffer transcendently for the extermination of hundreds of animal species or for the degradation of the oceans. Environmental guilt is collective, distributed unevenly among the people now living and those who have lived before, the wealthy and the poor, the developed and the aspiring. Without a personality to focus upon, ecological crisis presents merely a spectacle of catastrophe with none of the redemptive prospects of genuine tragic experience.

The culture that informed Sinus Block as he grew up had its roots in the tragic tradition and in the philosophical and religious premises that supported it. The assumption of human superiority to the processes of nature has justified human exploitation of nature without regard for the consequences to animals, plants, or the land. Human concern with a supernatural moral order has directed attention away from the natural environment and minimized its importance to human ethical life. The same moral order has tended to simplify complex relationships and reduce them to simple polarizations. Humanistic individualism has encouraged people to ignore the multiple dependencies necessary to the sustenance of life. The myopic search for personal identity and self-fulfillment has overwhelmed human responsibility to our own species and to the other creatures with whom we share the Earth.

4 * Hamlet and the Animals

As tragedy is ironic, so comedy is ambiguous. When the polarized conflicts essential to a tragic view of life begin to lose their power, they are replaced by a pluralized perspective that makes all value judgments seem uncertain. The gradual decline of a tragic view of the universe has proceeded rapidly since the Renaissance, but it was well under way by the time Shakespeare began writing in the late sixteenth century. In *Hamlet*, tragic modes of behavior and belief exist side by side with the comic, and the hero straddles the uncomfortable space between. Hamlet, like most twentieth-century people, is uncertain whether the world he lives in is a moral universe governed by dependable metaphysical values, or a biological environment that he shares on more or less equal terms with the other animals.

A central feature of the plot of *Hamlet* is the prince's apparent inability to act when action seems clearly to be called for. After meeting with the ghost of his murdered father early in the play, Hamlet knows what must be done and he swears bloody revenge. Impediments appear or are manufactured by Hamlet, however, so that by the middle of the play it appears doubtful if he is ever going to get on with the business. When everyone's patience is thin, Hamlet revives the violent expectations of his audience and his own flagging resolve with his mousetrap: the play within the play designed to illustrate the manner of his father's murder, to gain a telltale response from Claudius, and simultaneously to validate the ghost's story. It works too well, leaving Hamlet with no further excuse for delay and every reason in the world to take his revenge. "Now I could drink hot blood," he proclaims; given the circumstances, he may even mean it.

The audience has two more acts to wait, however, with only a minor murder (that of Polonius) to satisfy somewhat the accumulated bloodthirst. Abundant complications stall the inevitable violent revenge as the action is diverted to focus upon the queen, Polonius, a voyage to England, the death of Ophelia, squabbles with Laertes, and many lesser distractions of the brain.

The first small distraction is one of Hamlet's most inventive and properly admired manipulations. Immediately following the players' scene, when Hamlet is brimming with vengeful intent, his school friends Rosencrantz and Guildenstern arrive to ask him to talk to his upset mother. Moments later Polonius enters with the same request. The three message-bearers are all allied with the king and so represent the enemy, but all are personally harmless to Hamlet. There is no direct threat in their manner or intentions regarding him. One might expect Hamlet to brush all three aside or ignore them at such a moment—or, alternatively, perhaps to murder them on the spot if he is as worked up as he says he is. Instead, Hamlet attacks them with the weapons he controls best: metaphor, wit, and imagination.

When Guildenstern asks Hamlet to explain his strange behavior of late, Hamlet in turn asks Guildenstern to play a tune on one of the recorders left behind by the actors. Guildenstern confesses that he lacks musical skill, and Hamlet then drives home his point:

> Why, look you now, how unworthy a thing you make of me! You would play upon me, you would seem to know my stops, you would pluck out the heart of my mystery, you would sound me from my lowest note to the top of my compass—and there is much music, excellent voice, in this little organ—yet cannot you make it speak. 'Sblood, do you think I am easier to be played on than a pipe? Call me what instrument you will, though you can fret me, you cannot play upon me.

[3.2.347–355][1]

Guildenstern is effectively silenced by Hamlet's scorn, and says no more.

Polonius then enters with similar meddling in mind, but he is disarmed when Hamlet plays upon him like a pipe:

> HAMLET: Do you see yonder cloud that's almost in the shape of a camel?
> POLONIUS: By the mass, and 'tis like a camel indeed.
> HAMLET: Methinks it is like a weasel.
> POLONIUS: It is backed like a weasel.
> HAMLET: Or like a whale?
> POLONIUS: Very like a whale.
>
> [3.2.359–365]

Hamlet manipulates those who would manipulate him, expending his anger through verbal mockery rather than direct aggression. When he is at last alone, he weighs the hatred that is now confirmed within him and decides how to discharge it:

> 'Tis now the very witching time of night,
> When churchyards yawn and Hell itself breathes out
> Contagion to this world. Now I could drink hot blood,
> And do such bitter business as the day
> Would quake to look on. Soft! Now to my mother.
> O heart, lose not thy nature, let not ever
> The soul of Nero enter this firm bosom.
> Let me be cruel, not unnatural.
> I will speak daggers to her, but use none.
> My tongue and soul in this be hypocrites,
> How in my words somever she be shent,
> To give them seals never, my soul, consent.
>
> [3.2.370–381]

It is a pity that the two crucial words of Hamlet's conclusion, "shent" and "seals," have disappeared from general usage and so are lost upon most modern audiences. To shend is to berate or strongly reprove, and to seal in this case means to fulfill one's words with actions. The "bitter business" and "hot blood" that occupy Hamlet's mind early in the soliloquy have been transformed into nothing more dangerous than sharp language by its end. He will speak daggers but use none, as he has already demonstrated by his treatment of Guildenstern and Polonius. The late Harold Goddard, an American Shakespearean scholar, aptly summarized the theme of this sequence of scenes: "Scorn is a diluted form of murder."[2] Hamlet's preferred weapon throughout the remainder of the play is to be the word, not the sword.

Redirection of Aggression

Animal ethologists might say that Hamlet's verbal assault upon Guildenstern and Polonius is a "redirection" of aggressive impulses through substitution. It is a common feature of social life among animals that the purpose of intraspecific combat is to gain ascendancy over the adversary, not to destroy him. When animals with the capacity to kill members of their own species reach a point in their battles where death will likely ensue shortly, one combatant will frequently turn aside and ferociously attack some nearby harmless object, like a tree or shrub, or in some other way inhibit its killing behavior or expend it harmlessly. "Honor" among animals is often satisfied by the safe discharge of aggression as well as by its more lethal expressions, and battles normally end with maximum face-saving and minimum bloodletting. Slaughter is necessary among animals only for nutritional reasons; when status and the maintenance of social order are at stake, shame and ritualized aggression are more appropriate.

Animals that live by killing seldom kill their own kind, although they may fight with them frequently. Konrad Lorenz, one of the founders of the science of ethology, asserted that "there is no single organism capable of self-defence, in particular no large carnivore capable of killing large prey, which does not possess a quite particular system of inhibitions . . . preventing the killing of con-specifics."[3] Patterns of interspecific and intraspecific aggressive behavior differ markedly. The distinction between the two types of aggression is particularly pronounced among animals equipped with an anatomy designed for killing: "Where one species possesses very dangerous weapons such as teeth or claws, which could easily kill an opponent if they were used, special inhibiting mechanisms have usually evolved which prevent killing of the species member; often the entire fight has become transformed into a tournament. Only rarely do well-armed animals use their weapons against a conspecific without any inhibition."[4]

It is obviously necessary to the survival of any predatory species that predation not be applied to a conspecific, just as it is necessary that the stomachs of meat-eating animals be protected against self-digestion. The case is rather different among nonpredatory or unarmed animals, most of which seem to lack strong inhibitions against killing conspecifics, but these species are usually incapable of killing under natural circumstances.

Human Substitutes for Murder

It is not necessary to anthropomorphize animals or zoomorphize Hamlet to see a similarity in their use of redirection at a dangerous moment. Certainly many people who are less symbolically human than Hamlet use his technique often. Judges strike the gavel on their benches when they would like to crack the skulls of lawyers and defendants, and wives break glassware rather than their husbands' necks. It takes a very special effort of the mind to pursue a battle where death or serious injury are likely to result. Military men and dedicated partisans have long since perfected arguments to convince people to stand their ground in the face of death, but it seems clearly to be a form of behavior that is unnatural, since each human generation must afflict it anew upon the next. Given the opportunity, people generally shy away from killing their own kind in spite of all training to the contrary. When one is clearly trapped, fighting to the death may look as good as dying without a struggle, but if an alternative is available, the normal human reaction is to grab at it.

We may ask whether Hamlet is a member of a predatory species blessed with instinctual inhibitions against intraspecific murder. Unfortunately, he is not. Human anatomical equipment is not well designed for killing, and does not seem to be accompanied by strong, genetically controlled patterns of inhibition against attacking conspecifics. People have made up for their shortage of teeth, claws, poisons, horns, and antlers by technological inventiveness. The human capacity to kill is mostly a cultural invention, not a natural gift, so we lack the instinctual controls over our weapons that other dangerous animals have. Instinct did not prevent Claudius from pouring poison in his brother's ear, and Laertes was instantly ready to shed vengeful blood when he heard that his father Polonius had been slain. Like our weapons, human inhibitory controls depend upon culture more than instinct.

Hamlet's inherited cultural morality tells him that murder in his situation is proper and appropriate. Somewhere within him, however, is a force that resists and looks for alternatives. He creates redirections with his mind when his instincts fail to supply them. Hamlet is an anomaly among heroes because of his strong aversion to lethal violence, although his evasive behavior would seem perfectly normal if it were observed in a wolf.

It is true, however, that human aggressive passions are capable of being discharged short of murder. We do have some basic distaste for killing members of our own species, whether its source is genetic or cultural. And harmless or symbolic violence can sometimes release us from the grip of destructive hate, as literary tragedy is thought to do in the Aristotelian theory of catharsis. We seem to share these features with many animals, particularly those complex enough to live a social existence where they must frequently compete with their own kind.

But is it therefore reasonable to conclude that Hamlet's actions following the mousetrap scene are explicable in the same terms as those of a moose who attacks a willow bush rather than another moose? So obvious and simple an explanation would surely have occurred to someone long ago and the problem of interpreting *Hamlet* need not have filled so many dreary books. There is nothing obvious or simple about either Hamlet or the moose. The mystery lies in the wonder that such a thing as redirected aggression should exist at all. But it does, and what remains is to consider the further complications arising from the great diversity of its manifestations. Hamlet's verbal murder of his school chum is more sophisticated than a wife breaking crockery, as the wife is more complex than the moose who suddenly hates willows. All are redirected aggression, and all serve to affirm the value of life above the values of honor and exclusive dominance.

Comic and Tragic Aggression

Seeking substitutes for dangerous aggression is unheroic and anti-tragic. It is a form of action more closely associated with comedy than with tragedy, with the avoidance of suffering rather than with noble acceptance of it. It is the behavior of Falstaff who feigns death rather than risk battle, or of Don Quixote who attacks windmills and sheep as if they were giants and armies, or of Joseph Heller's Yossarian in *Catch-22* who makes "evasive action" his moral principle of survival when faced with an enemy bent upon destroying him. Comic heroes consistently devote their energies and imaginative resources to finding alternatives to mortal combat, and are characteristically willing to endure humiliation rather than to kill or be killed. Temporary avoidance of death is a basic goal of comic action; the substitution of nonlethal for lethal combat is its technique.

Throughout most of the play, Hamlet tries to find comic resolutions to his problems. This hopeless search largely accounts for his seemingly inappropriate delay in taking revenge. His initial response to the ghost's demand for revenge is to "put an antic disposition on," permitting him to proceed by dissimulation rather than by direct aggressive action. From this point until the final scene of the play, Shakespeare presents a complicated series of scenes of aggression played skillfully by Hamlet on a verbal and symbolic level. The enemy Claudius and his allies—Rosencrantz and Guildenstern, Polonius, and Gertrude— are one by one verbally slain. Guildenstern and Polonius feel the sharpness of Hamlet's tongue in act 3, and such scenes recur with these characters at several points in the play. Gertrude is reduced to tears of shame and frustration by her son's lecture on the immorality of her remarriage. The most powerful mock-aggression of all is staged for Claudius in the mousetrap scene, with Hamlet interpreting the action so that the point will not be missed by the king. Of this scene, Goddard has said, "The play is nothing but a contrivance for murder on the mental plane."[5] Even simple Ophelia is symbolically destroyed by her lover ("Get thee to a nunnery"), and she never recovers her balance. Hamlet has been filled with aggressive passion by the legacy from his father, and his action throughout the play is a desperate search for means to discharge that aggression by finding substitutes for murder.

Incidental Victims

Hamlet successfully avoids confronting the genuine object of his aggression, Claudius, until the final scene of the play. Meanwhile, his hate proves fatal to others despite his attempts to redirect it. When Rosencrantz and Guildenstern are dispatched to escort Hamlet to England, where the king has arranged secretly for his execution, Hamlet deftly turns the tables and arranges for his companions to be killed according to the king's plan. Hamlet recognizes that the deaths of Rosencrantz and Guildenstern are incidental to the larger conflict between himself and the king:

'Tis dangerous when the baser nature comes
Between the pass and fell incensed points
Of mighty opposites.

[5.2.60–62]

The same explanation fits Polonius and Ophelia, who also die as unintended victims of Hamlet's aggression toward Claudius. Both are relatively innocent observers of the combat between Hamlet and the king, rather like willows smashed at the scene of battle between bull moose. Ophelia's adolescent perplexity becomes insanity and leads to her death as she fails to cope with the bewildering events around her. Her father Polonius, as Gertrude describes him, is a "good old man" despite his habit of meddling in others' affairs. His inappropriate presence in the queen's chambers at the moment when Hamlet's aggressive passion is at its height (immediately following the mousetrap scene) results in his death by reflex action, not by design.

Hamlet kills Polonius without seeing him, and not as a man but as a rat. Had Polonius been visible as a human being instead of hiding furtively behind a curtain, Hamlet would surely have attacked as usual with words rather than with his rapier, constrained by his consistent aversion against intraspecific murder. Hamlet's distraught mind instantly created an image of an animal competitor, the rat, which could legitimately be killed.

Pseudospeciation

Hamlet's casual murder of Polonius has its counterpart in animal behavior in another sense. Behavioral inhibitions preventing conspecifics from destroying one another occasionally break down. Under great stress, wolves have been known to kill other wolves, and overpopulated rats sometimes kill other rats. The late psychologist Erik Erikson named this phenomenon "pseudospeciation," or the adoption of interspecific behavioral patterns of aggression inappropriately applied to a conspecific.[6] The clearest examples of pseudospeciation are to be found in the history of human culture, where this remarkable behavior has become institutionalized. Hamlet's cry, "How now! A rat? Dead, for a ducat, dead!" as he kills Polonius is a small but revealing example of the coincidence of pseudospeciation and murder among humans.

An early and compelling example of pseudospeciation occurs near the end of Homer's *Iliad*, where the heroes Achilles and Hector at last confront one another for battle. Hector has been chased three times around the walls of Troy before he finally confronts Achilles in a last vain attempt to reason with his adversary in a civilized fashion. Achilles' answer is a classic example of the human use of pseudospeciation:

> Hektor, argue me no arguments. I cannot forgive you.
> As there are no trustworthy oaths between men and lions,
> nor wolves and lambs have spirit that can be brought to agreement
> but forever these hold feelings of hate for each other,
> so there can be no love between you and me, nor shall there be
> oaths between us, but one or the other must fall before then
> to glut with his blood Ares the god who fights under the shield's guard.[7]

Achilles insists that he is a predator and Hector is his prey of another species; therefore, presumably no constraints to aggression can apply. It is a simple logical trick that allows Achilles to ignore the fact that he and his adversary are both humans and so at least theoretically subject to "trustworthy oaths" limiting or ritualizing aggression. Wolves, of course, do not normally treat other wolves as prey, nor do lions prey upon lions; both behave toward their conspecifics in a relatively polite manner compared to their treatment of prey species, except in those rare instances of pseudospeciation when they seem to forget that they are dealing with one of their own kind.

Identifying the enemy as an animal is an ancient technique of murderers and military propagandists. Jews were dogs or swine in Hitler's Germany, and Chinese are said to think of Americans as (paper) tigers. If an appropriate animal species does not seem to fit the enemy, humans have often invented new nonhuman species names to disguise their conspecific foes: wop, honky, gook, nigger, spic, and the host of other pejorative names applied to ethnic groups are pseudospecific categories long used to justify violent behavior. The purpose and effect of these inventions is always to deprive people of the rights and protections normally accorded to other human beings.

Blood Revenge

The tradition of blood revenge advocated by the ghost of Hamlet's father is also a cultural invention, not an instinctual pattern shared alike by people and animals. No counterpart for the long chains of family feuding over many generations described in tragic literature is to be found in animal behavior. Genetic heritage does not seem to affirm the biblical pattern of "visiting the iniquity of the fathers upon the children of the third and fourth generation," nor is there any sign of an animal instinct compelling offspring to avenge the deaths of their parents. Human language and memory alone make it possible to retain and transmit hatreds and fears long after the occasions that produced them have passed.

Hamlet's prolonged inaction is remarkable because it is an implicit rejection of the morally correct norms of his culture that support blood revenge. Shakespeare has provided within the play an example of "proper" (culturally approved) revenge behavior so that we may gauge how far Hamlet's response is from normal. When young Laertes hears that his father has been killed, he promptly collects a band of supporters who proclaim him king, and with his following he bursts into the throne room demanding instant vengeance no matter what the cost:

> I dare damnation. To this point I stand,
> That both the worlds I give to negligence,
> Let come what comes; only I'll be revenged
> Most throughly for my father.
>
> [4.5.131–135]

That is the way a hero is supposed to be, ready to sacrifice his chances at heaven, the welfare of the state, and any lives including his own that may be required by the code of honor. There are no parallels to animal behavior in Laertes' action, for his vengeance is unknown outside the context of human culture. Although he proves to have little talent for the role of hero, Laertes at least affirms the traditional model of heroic revenge that is typical of his cultural tradition.

By comparison, Hamlet is a poor example of heroic values. In his influential essay on *Hamlet* in the novel *Wilhelm Meister's Apprenticeship* (1796), Goethe described Hamlet as "a lovely, pure, noble, and most moral nature, without the strength of nerve which forms a hero," and found in his story "the effects of a great action laid upon a soul unfit for the performance of it."[8] Had Hamlet lived up to the heroic expectations of his culture, he would presumably have murdered Claudius as promptly as possible and assumed the throne for himself rather than experimenting with alternatives as he does. Hamlet's attempt to find a comic resolution to his problems mocks the tragic and heroic ideals of Western civilization.

Hamlet's Gamesmanship

Hamlet tries at every opportunity to convert actions into words, violence into argument, murder into a game. He thus reverses the usual processes of tragic action, which normally move from word to deed, argument to battle, threats to murder. He is a master of redirected aggression, and his success at avoiding serious violence provides much of the substance of the play. In the end, of course, he must fail and the audience must be satisfied, not simply because of the conventions of the theater but because Hamlet's evasive strategy is unintelligible and unacceptable to his fellow humans. It would make immediate sense to most predatory animals and evoke from them a like response, but among humans it merely inspires the escalation of violence.

While Hamlet manufactures games, his opponents are inventing plans for action. The final scene of the play begins with a duel that Hamlet sees as an athletic contest, but which to Claudius and Laertes is a pretext for murder. Hamlet accepts the invitation to "play with Laertes" in good sporting faith, hoping to win the duel on points; "if not, I will gain nothing but my shame." Life is not at stake so far as Hamlet is concerned, although he does have a vague intuition that this will not be an ordinary game and confesses to Horatio, "thou wouldst not think how ill all's here about my heart." Claudius and Laertes, meanwhile, are preparing for murder and filling the athletic site with instruments of death: an unbated point for Laertes' rapier, poison on the blade, and poison in the wine. In the duel that follows, Hamlet's entire strategy of life as an infinite game is pitted against the tradition of life as tragic action, and Hamlet of course loses even though he is a better fencer than Laertes. Hamlet is forced to abandon his comic behavior of redirected violence and to adopt the tragic pattern of violent heroics that can lead only to violent death. The final result is the destruction of Denmark's most important people: king, queen, prince, and courtier.

Social Responses to Aggression

Tragic literature has frequently demonstrated that prevailing cultural traditions are dangerous and destructive to the welfare of the human species. Aeschylus was as sensitive to the problem in the fifth century B.C. as Shakespeare was in the seventeenth. Aeschylus's trilogy, *The Oresteia*, examines the theme of blood revenge in detail, searching desperately for some way to avoid the endless chain of destruction as each new generation of leaders assumes responsibility for avenging the wrongs done to their parents. Thanks to the unique human capacity for preserving information, revenge can become a traditional pattern of cultural behavior for an indefinite period, causing the destruction of many lives.

In the final play of the trilogy, *The Eumenides*, Aeschylus celebrates the Greek invention of distributive justice. Personal blood revenge is replaced by a jury of twelve citizens that acts in the name of society as a whole and decides issues of right and wrong according to the welfare of the people rather than by the relative destructive power of the disputants. Aeschylus presents this advance as a triumph of Greek rationality over primordial instinct (Apollo over the Furies). Had he known more about animal ethology, Aeschylus might well have regarded distributive justice as a victory of animal instinct over a destructive cultural tradition.

A legal trial is a communal form of redirected aggression. In the interest of social welfare and survival, it restricts combat between antagonists to a verbal and symbolic level, and it imposes punishments mostly in the form of humiliations and restrictions on free behavior rather than death or physical injury. The long debate over the appropriateness of the death penalty and other "cruel and unusual" punishments is a legacy of cultural blood revenge, which the Greeks thought they had ended some twenty-five centuries ago. Deliberate execution of deviant or dangerous conspecifics for purposes of punishment is to be found in only one species, our own.

Animal societies, like some human societies, do occasionally assume group responsibility for preventing battles between strong leaders when a risk of death or serious injury is present. I once sat on the edge of a Bavarian marsh with Konrad Lorenz, watching his flock of some two hundred greylag geese when a serious fight broke out between two strong males, Percy and Ado. It was a grudge match, preceded by several months of skirmishing between the two prominent geese, but this time it went too far. With

Ado's beak firmly clamped upon Percy's wing, Percy was helplessly receiving terrible blows from his assailant's heavy wings. Percy would not have survived long had he not managed to take sanctuary under the bench upon which Dr. Lorenz and I were seated. The other geese were extremely excited, and several large ganders were preparing to interfere with the fight before Percy had reached our bench. Lorenz explained that he had observed such behavior on several occasions during serious fights between rivals, when "all the courageous ganders converged on the battle and proceeded to beat the fighters until they were separated." Lorenz also added that during such fights, "I have to keep myself in leash; I find it difficult not to interfere."[9] The citizens watching helplessly from the walls of Troy must have felt similarly when Achilles and Hector fought to the death, and the courtiers of Denmark might have tried to save some of their royalty if the final scene of *Hamlet* had not moved so fast. The social impulse to find alternatives to lethal aggression is as strong as the private need, and it is shared by animals and humans alike, although people often suppress such impulses as animals cannot.

An Animal with Choices

Neither Hamlet nor the humanity that he represents is degraded simply by being compared with animals, nor are animals exalted thereby. Hamlet demonstrates, however, how impossible it is to be at the same time both a good man according to the criteria of tragedy, and a good human animal according to the requirements of nature. Even intellectual and imaginative gifts as great as Hamlet's often do not serve the best individual interests or those of the species. Try as we may to use our mental ability to fulfill our comic instincts for survival, we are unlikely to succeed if we remain, like Hamlet, trapped in a cultural tradition that affirms the supremacy of the tragic point of view.

It is important to remember that alternatives do exist within the Western cultural and literary traditions. Hamlet's mode of action is not the only one available. There are others that make use of the human mind to affirm and to satisfy human needs more successfully. These modes will be examined in the remaining chapters.

5 * The Pastoral and the Picaresque

The world has often seemed like a scary place for people. Ours is not the first period in history to notice that there is much corruption in social and political structures, that conventional moralities do not address our real problems, that there are too many people for comfort, that the technologies that promised us ease have also damaged our lives and environments, and that crime and violence are escalating. It is not that the world is itself malevolent or that the gods are angry, for most modern people are well aware that the threats to human well-being are of our own making.

As people have invented their unhappiness, so they have invented means for relief. Since the Renaissance began to unfold the new ages of humanism and technology, Western culture has sought to evade their destructive consequences by using a variety of psychological and intellectual devices. Pastoral and picaresque literature represent two important patterns of response to an unacceptable world. Both terms are commonly applied to conventional literary genres, but both also identify modes of human behavior and systems of human values. Both are currently in use as models for human responses to contemporary social, intellectual, and natural environments.

The choice between them is therefore of some usefulness in deciding what to do about the difficult world around us.

The pastoral tradition is the older of the two, and its historical credentials are impressive. Some find its roots in the Genesis account of the Garden of Eden, where the proper human environment appears as a fertile and pleasant natural setting characterized by peace and innocence. But the Roman poet Virgil of the first century B.C. gets credit for perfecting the literary form of the pastoral poem with its conventions of sylvan glades, peaceful animals, and happy shepherds who live in love and kinship with nature. Virgil's pastoral was revived at the Renaissance and has since been the model for countless literary works and a major influence upon modern attitudes toward both nature and human society.

The picaresque tradition has no such classical pedigree. Scholars differ over its literary origins, its definition, and the kind of evidence that might be needed to interpret it. There is general agreement that the term derives from the Spanish *pícaro*, "rogue," and that the genre comprises tales about socially deprived people. The first clear example of the form is the anonymous little book *Lazarillo de Tormes*, which appeared in Spain in 1554. *Lazarillo* is the story of a young man's adventures as he struggles to survive in a hostile world that seems bent upon destroying him. To endure, he must adapt himself somehow to the given conditions of his environment, however many rules of decorum and ethics must be ignored in the process. The picaresque, at its origins, is a mode of survival against odds in a world that is hostile or indifferent.

Simply put, escape from the mad world or adaptation to its conditions are the choices offered by the pastoral and picaresque modes. Both presuppose some necessary relationship between human social and biological environments, but differ in their assessment of that relationship. The pastoral looks longingly at biological nature as an alternative to society, while the picaresque sees society itself as a natural environment—a wilderness. Civilization has been in a perpetual state of social and biological crisis at least since the Renaissance. Perhaps these two literary traditions can help to reveal whether they are in fact two different crises, or only one.

The Pastoral Fantasy

The pastoral tradition is rooted in imperial Rome, although it has significant antecedents in Hellenistic Greece and is reinforced by weighty influences from the Hebrew Old Testament. It was Virgil, however, who set the pastoral tone of greatest influence. Virgil's *Eclogues*, published in 37 B.C., reflects the weariness of sensitive Romans to the excesses and injustices of their society and their quest for solace and sense in a rural setting. "Lo, to what wretched pass has civil discord brought us," exclaims Meliboeus in the first *Eclogue*.[1] Expelled from his farm by war and its political aftermath, he laments the future and admires his friend who has managed to retain land to grow old on: "Happy in thy old age, here, amid familiar streams and holy springs thou wilt woo the coolness of the shade."[2] Rural repose is contrasted throughout the *Eclogues* with "the thankless town," the symbol of anxiety and misery. Virgil's pastorals show people being oppressed by urban life, but comforted by nature.

Rome inspired many besides Virgil to seek relief on the farm, and for many of the same reasons that move modern urbanites to take refuge in the country. Romans of the first and second centuries often found in their city the same features that cause New Yorkers and Los Angelenos to dream of pastoral settings. The Roman satirist Decimus Junius Juvenalis, in his *Third Satire* (ca. A.D. 110–130), presents a familiar catalogue of urban ills: degrading poverty in the ghettos, high taxes, inflated prices for poor goods and services, corrupt government, crime and vice in the streets, poor schools and wicked teachers, pressures of social conformity, traffic congestion, police brutality, and environmental pollution. "Rome, the great sewer" seems to Juvenal beyond redemption, and his only solution is to go back to the farm:

> Tear yourself from the games, and get a place
>   in the country!
> One little Latian town, like Sora, say,
>   or Frusino,
> Offers a choice of homes, at a price you pay here,
>   in one year,
> Renting some hole in the wall. Nice houses, too,
>   with a garden,

Springs bubbling up from the grass, no need for
    windlass or bucket,
Plenty to water your flowers, if they need it,
    without any trouble.
Live there, fond of your hoe, an independent
    producer,
Willing and able to feed a hundred good vegetarians.
Isn't it something, to feel, wherever you are,
    how far off,
You are a monarch? At least, lord of a
    single lizard.[3]

Juvenal's rhetoric, like that of contemporary suburban real estate develop-
ers, stresses the goodness of life in the country, and the final lines reveal
another familiar motivation: It is better to be lord of a single lizard than a
victim of urban exploitation. The city degrades people and the country re-
stores their sense of power and dignity; in the city we are controlled, but
in the country we control. A rural setting symbolizes both the purity of
nature and the power of people, a conjunction whose paradoxes were present two thousand years ago. Juvenal was hardly a pastoral poet, although
he did share Virgil's belief that amid flocks and fields, trees and birds, one
might find both the spiritual peace and the personal satisfaction that cities
couldn't offer.

The pastoral goal has always been to find in rural nature an alternative
to the ills of civilization. With the decline of Rome, pastoral literature and
its attitudes became scarce, perhaps for lack of oppressive cities from which
escape was needed. But when the cities arose again with the early Renaissance, pastoral values were revived to meet the needs of harried humanists.
Both the pastoral literary genre perfected by Virgil and the antiurban conventions of jaded Romans such as Juvenal seemed to express perfectly the
sentiments of many of the new people of the Renaissance.

Disease was one of the more dramatic evils of city life in late medieval
and Renaissance Europe. Epidemics of black plague were environmental
disasters partly attributable to environmental pollution, humanly induced
ecological imbalance, and overcrowding in the newly great cities. When the
plague struck Florence in 1348, the aristocratic young men and women of
Giovanni Boccaccio's collection of tales, the *Decameron*, sought refuge from

death and social disorder in a genteel tour of the Italian countryside where they told one another risqué stories to pass the time. Although the *Decameron* is not properly a pastoral tale, its framework shows the pastoral motivation to flee from the pain and danger of the city to the solace and pleasure of rural life.

Boccaccio's introduction paints a grim picture of the diseased city where "everyone felt doomed and had abandoned his property," where "the authority of human and divine laws almost disappeared," and where "people cared no more for dead men than we care for dead goats."[4] The alternative to all this misery, sought out by Boccaccio's young people, is a rural garden described in traditional pastoral images: "The sight of this garden, of its beautiful plan, of the plants, and the fountain and the little streams flowing from it, so much pleased the ladies and three young men that they said, if Paradise could be formed on earth, it could be given no other form than that of this garden, nor could any further beauty be added to it."[5] The young people weave garlands from the garden plants, listen to the twenty different birds who serenade them, and delight in the hundreds of beautiful rabbits, goats, deer, and "many other kinds of harmless animals running about as if they were tame."[6] To the classical image of a domesticated rural landscape composed of beautiful plants and harmless animals, the Renaissance can add the dimension of moral innocence that derives from the biblical Garden of Eden and the medieval view of heaven as a divinely created pastoral scene. To the pastoral eye, society is bewilderingly complicated and dangerous while nature is beautifully simple and congenial.

The pastoral flourishes in times of urban crisis, or in those periods often called decadent, when traditional forms and rituals of society have become inappropriate but continue to hold the allegiance of large numbers of people who can find no alternative. One result is a general sense, especially among privileged and intellectual people, that the world is unmanageable, unintelligible, and doomed to self-destruction. Those who have the means to escape begin to look for places to hide from the foreseeable apocalypse, either in a new physical setting or in their fantasies. The pastoral tradition provides both.

Rural life seems rational at such times because it is thought to be governed by natural rather than human laws. Crops sprout, mature, and are harvested for human sustenance in dependable cycles. Animals graze placidly in their pastures without all the jostling and conflicts generated among people who crowd the marketplaces. And the rustic farmer who supervises nature's nourishing processes appears to be a contributing part of the sensible system surrounding him, unlike his socially alienated urban brother. To a tired and frustrated aristocrat, agriculture is a symbol of tranquility and order, God's image of what life should be like everywhere.

Nostalgia for a lost Golden Age is satisfied in part by the discovery in the present of simplified forms of order in agriculture and gardening. Agriculture becomes symbolic of both structural integrity and moral innocence. Eden, after all, was merely a small farm characterized by abundance, purity, and simplicity until its agrarian tenants noticed the existence of some awkwardly polarized contradictions, like good and evil, male and female, obedience and rebellion, and as a result were sent off to build cities where such conflicts belong. The pastoral hope is to reclaim that lost simplicity by escaping present complexity, whether its imagery is that of a classical Golden Age, a biblical garden, a rural landscape, a national park, or merely a suburban lawn with its small vegetable and flower garden to represent the good and natural life in contrast to the evils of civilization.

The pastoral impulse is utopian in its assumption that suffering and chaos are unnecessary and that strategies that will overcome such ills are possible, indeed natural. Adam's unfortunate choice to leave the garden behind was also an abandonment of reason, of common sense, and of orderly administrative structure, but God has generously permitted vestiges of the original plan to persist in the form of farms and gardens that people may imitate in order to regain Eden. If society can only be organized according to the proper principles of organic gardening, peace and stability will surely follow. The utopian vision, like the pastoral, sees nature at work in agriculture and seeks to reproduce the fertility, peacefulness, durability, simplicity, and moral innocence of gardens among the social structures of humanity.

Ebenezer Howard, the influential nineteenth-century English landscape architect and city planner, built his utopian Garden City upon a pastoral foundation:

> The key to the problem how to restore the people to the land—that beautiful land of ours, with its canopy of sky, the air that blows upon it, the sun that warms it, the rain and dew that moisten it—the very embodiment of Divine love for man—is indeed a *Master Key*, for it is the key to a portal through

which, even when scarce ajar, will be seen to pour a flood of light on the problems of intemperance, of excessive toil, of restless anxiety, of grinding poverty—the true limits of Governmental interference, ay, and even the relations of man to the Supreme Power.[7]

Howard's alternative to the pain and degradation of city life, like Juvenal's, is the garden. The difference is that Howard wants to rebuild cities to incorporate the virtues of gardens, not merely to escape from the city. Howard had hope for humanity. He was confident that the influence of the garden upon the city would provide a solution to psychological, social, political, and even theological problems common to urban environments. His utopian vision sought relief in fantasies of future gardens, not merely in a change of geography or a return to a previous golden-age garden.

The United States may be the world's largest-scale utopian experiment in creating a nation on the model of a pastoral garden. Many of its earliest settlers looked upon the new land as a green refuge from the oppression they had suffered in European cities. The American pastoral ideal has been studied in detail by Leo Marx in his book *The Machine in the Garden*. Marx traces the pervasive pastoral strain in American thought and shows the painful contradictions that developed as the American garden was gradually transformed into an industrialized farm, then into a national factory: "Beginning in Jefferson's time, the cardinal image of American aspirations was a rural landscape, a well-ordered green garden magnified to continental size."[8] An agricultural America must be both beautiful and morally pure, for, according to Jefferson, "those who labor in the earth are the chosen people of God . . . whose breasts he has made his peculiar deposit for substantial and genuine virtue."[9] Marx also shows that the snake of industrialism that was to corrupt the garden was also known to Jefferson. Foreign competition and the War of 1812 forced America to abandon its gardening project in order to defend itself. Jefferson knew that the garden would never be the same again: "Our enemy has indeed the consolation of Satan on removing our first parents from Paradise: from a peaceable and agricultural nation, he makes us a military and manufacturing one."[10] With the machine in power, the garden was doomed.

The conflict between the pastoral garden and the industrial machine is a fundamental polarity of American thought that has tormented Americans from the beginning. As the machine has achieved greater dominance, the

American garden has gradually disappeared, and with it American hopes for realizing a pastoral utopia of peace and purity.

Unfortunately, pastoral gardens are usually made by the same machines that will eventually destroy them. In order to maintain the human dominance and safety required by pastoral values, it is necessary to assert human technological advantage over nature. Predatory or dangerous animal competitors must be exterminated or expelled; poisonous, ugly, or inedible plants must be rooted out; land must be cultivated and sown to nourishing crops or used as pasture for fattening human sources of meat. Whether the machine is the hoe that Juvenal's Roman is so fond of, the rifle and railroad that cleared the prairies of buffalo, or the bulldozers, chemicals, and irrigation systems of modern farming, the machine is an indispensable part of the pastoral garden, for it alone gives people the power to civilize nature. Gardens are not images of nature, but of the human management of nature.

When anthropologists talk about "the pastoral age" they are not referring to a poetic period, but to the stage of human evolution when plants and animals were domesticated, thus encouraging permanent settlements and changing humanity's nutritional relationship with the environment. That kind of pastoralism freed people from the need to hunt and pick berries, and made it possible to pay attention to such things as theology, politics, philosophy, art, and science. Pastoral poetry expresses a longing for this early stage of civilization when agriculture had given people leisure and sufficiency, but before the development of elaborate social and political structures. What the pastoral tradition calls "nature" is merely simplified civilization. No pastoral poet ever gets nostalgic thinking about Paleolithic hunters or australopithecine apes, nor does he long for unimproved wilderness or for violent aspects of natural processes.

The pastoral symphony is a thoroughly domesticated score orchestrated solely around human themes. Its central images—farm, garden, pasture—show nature at the service of the farmer and husbandman. Pastoral scenes include plants valuable for their nutritional or ornamental qualities and animals that have been tamed for human use, such as sheep, cattle, and dogs. The only wild animals are noncompetitors, like songbirds whose music is assumed to be designed for human entertainment. Dangerous or competitive plants and animals are strictly excluded. The pastoral landscape does not permit thistles or loco weed, wolves, lions, eagles, vultures, mosquitos, or poisonous spiders. And when a snake appears in such a garden, it is a sign that the place has been corrupted already. Pastoral values glorify anthropocentric agriculture and rigidly reject the possibility that wild nature has any independent integrity.

Pastoral literature demonstrates the futility that must result from the full exploration of pastoral motives. The pastoral hero is never an image of human success or greatness, and he never achieves what he has been longing for. As his career begins in fear, self-pity, or self-indulgence, so in the end we are likely to see him "either dead or totally alienated from society, alone and powerless, like the evicted shepherd of Virgil's eclogue."[11] The pastoral epiphany is a recognition that neither human society nor wilderness is a suitable environment for people, and that the garden, trying to mediate between the two, merely separates us from other humans and from nature.

Inherent contradictions in pastoral values lead typically to frustration and despair. The sensitive aristocrat who turns toward Arcadia and away from Rome often discovers that Rome is really within him. Although he can leave behind the fearsome environment of civilization and its cities, yet the psyche of civilization remains to guide his responses to nature. He cannot reject civilization without rejecting his own humanness, so he seeks a compromise in the halfway house of a pastoral Arcadia, somewhere midway between the horrors of wilderness and the horrors of the city. His choice of the garden-farm is this exact midpoint, a place of mediation between nature and civilization, but also the point where the two worlds make contact and where both continually tug at him. His fear of wilderness is as intense as his fear of cities, and the garden merely intensifies the contrast without providing a resolution. In his total alienation from both worlds, his only response is self-pity and despair at ever resolving the contradictions that he has now discovered to be internal as well as environmental. He cannot even achieve tragedy, for he has not risked enough. The end of the pastoral cycle is pathos.

Picaresque Strategies

The picaresque world is a natural system in which humans are one of the animal species. The picaro suffers from no conflict between society and nature simply because he sees society as one of the many forms of natural order. He objects to the society into which he is born no more than wolves or ants or whales object to theirs, and like these animals, he tries merely to adapt himself to his circumstances in the interest of his own survival. He does not altruistically strive for the welfare of all humanity, but merely lives his life as well as he can with little regard for distant idealisms. He is so completely absorbed as a participant in life that it never occurs to him to be a critic of it, or to escape into fantasies.

Picaresque nature is not a garden, but a wilderness. Its most obvious features are multiplicity and diversity, for within the picaresque world everything is tied to everything else according to complex interdependencies that defy simplification. Pain and pleasure are equally real, as are birth and death, peace and war, hunger and a full belly, love and hate. To attend to only one side of these polarities while rejecting the other would be to distort the truth, which the picaro knows he must not do if he hopes to endure. Instead, he takes each as it comes (often they come mixed) and deals with it according to its demands, enjoying the pleasant and enduring the painful as best he can. His world is an ecosystem and he is but one small organism within it. How he fits into the whole or what its purpose may be are beyond him, but he doesn't worry much about such questions.

The picaro's birth is generally obscure, often illegitimate, suggesting both his lack of social status and the absence of any sense of continuity with the past. The chaotic social environment in which he grows up has no niche prepared for him, and he soon discovers that he must create whatever success he can from the rawest of materials at hand. Early in life he goes on his own. His experiences quickly awaken him to the realization that no one will help him, that there is no obvious plan or order in the world, and that his survival or failure will depend upon his own inventiveness.

Lazarillo de Tormes, the Spanish novel already mentioned, is the prototype for later picaresque novels. Its hero, Lazarillo, is tricked and beaten by his first master and promptly achieves the realization that defines the picaresque perspective: "It is full time for me to open mine eyes, yea, and to provide and seek mine own advantage, considering that I am alone without any help."[12] Eyes wide open upon the world around him, looking to avoid danger and to exploit advantages, the picaro lives life as an infinite game played with the world, the only prizes for which are more life and an occasional hearty laugh. Lazarillo and the picaresque nonheroes modeled upon him live in risky play with their surrounding social order.

The picaresque hero perceives that the world is particularly dangerous to those who are poor, weak, or defenseless. The high moral and cultural values mouthed by powerful people are merely platitudes that do not in fact govern their actions and so they cannot be taken seriously. Those who live within the established social order are well fed, pious, educated in abstractions but often stupid in practical matters, and vindictive to all who do not conform to their ideals. The picaro is an outsider to this system, practical, clever, amoral, self-sufficient, and dedicated to making do by the best means available. Staying alive is his most important purpose, and having a good time comes second. He does not rebel against his society, nor does he try to reform it or escape from it. Rather, he looks for weaknesses and loopholes in the system that he can use to his own advantage.

The picaro notes the chaotic complexity of society as keenly as his pastoral counterpart, but he reasons that he must meet it by becoming more complex himself, not by seeking simplicity. He learns early in his career that the elaborate mechanisms of social order do not serve his basic human needs, but that does not lead him to hate society. It simply means that he will have to assume full responsibility for his own welfare and that he can expect no help from others. The picaro is alone, not in the lofty and self-indulgent way of the pastoral hero, but in the modest manner of one who simply assumes that no one really cares about him. The problems around him seem too great to be solved or even understood, but since they were not of his making he need not feel guilty. He does need to live in the world that is defined by these problems, however, so he needs intelligence and wit.

William Faulkner's novel *The Reivers* is marginally a picaresque novel. A statement made by the narrator of that story could serve as a definition of picaresque intelligence: "I rate mules second only to rats in intelligence, the mule followed in order by cats, dogs, and horses last—assuming of course that you accept my definition of intelligence: which is the ability to cope with environment yet still retain at least something of personal liberty."[13] The intelligence of mules, rats, and picaresque heroes is directed not toward puzzling out the rational elegance of pastoral utopias, but toward coping with the given circumstances of daily life. There is little room for nostalgia, fantasy, or abstract intellectual speculation in the mind of the picaro, for he is occupied with present actions and events, and with the maintenance of his own precarious liberty.

The picaro (or occasionally, picara) is thus an opportunist rather than an escapist, a person of wit rather than of contemplation, a realist rather than an idealist. His commitment to endure must often be served by breaking or ignoring the laws and rules of his society. He is often an outlaw and vulgar in the eyes of society's aristocrats.

Defensive Strategies

The world in which the picaro must make his way is often at war. Two picaresque war novels from different historical periods will illustrate the consistency of the picaresque genre: *Simplicius Simplicissimus* by the seventeenth-century German writer Johann Jacob Christoffel von Grimmelshausen, and *Catch-22* by the twentieth-century American novelist Joseph Heller. Grimmelshausen's *Simplicissimus* and Heller's *Catch-22* represent typical picaresque responses to the questions that war always raises: How can one live in a time of total social disruption, and what is one to do about the omnipresent threat of injury and death? The picaresque answers are always the same: Adapt to circumstances and take evasive action.

What the black plague was to Boccaccio, the Thirty Years' War was to Grimmelshausen. All Europe suffered near total collapse of civilized amenities, ostensibly over the resolution of religious differences between Protestants and Catholics. Grimmelshausen's picaresque novel begins with scenes of carnage and brutality that define the world in which young Simplicius must make his way. "This introductory entertainment almost spoiled my desire to see the world," remarks Simplicius after witnessing the brutal destruction of his village by a cavalry troop: "If this is the way things are, the wilderness is far more attractive."[14] Although he tries to hide in the forest, events always force him back into human company, where he begins to learn the tricks of survival.

Like most picaresque novels, *Simplicissimus* represents a young man's initiation and education. Simplicius's first teacher is a minister whose message is that "the foolish world wants to be fooled. Use what intelligence they have left you . . . for your own advantage" (80). Intelligence in service of deception is the picaro's basic strategy for survival. But the picaro deceives only so that he may save himself, never intentionally to injure others. Simplicius adopts whatever disguises seem appropriate in order to avoid trouble. His protective coloring makes him into a court jester, a minister, a soldier, a doctor, or an animal as his situation warrants. Each role saves him from some danger, and each teaches him something new by providing a fresh perspective upon events. Although he deceives others, he never gives in to the temptation to take his own disguises seriously.

The picaro does not treat his fantasies as if they were realities, as pastoral heroes tend to do, but regards each new role as one possibility out of the many available to him, useful for solving a particular problem and perhaps interesting for the new insight it may offer, but in no way a limitation to be accepted. Picaresque life is not lived in search of the One True Way, but is rather an endless series of roles to be played in response to ever-changing circumstances.

Simplicius often compares himself to animals and even adopts animal disguises. He becomes a goose to avoid punishment, and later enjoys for some time the role of calf. As a talking animal he lectures his masters on the virtues of animals, praising them for their moderation, responsiveness to environment, and peacefulness compared to humans. Animals are congenial images to the picaro, for like him they live in the present and are not subject to self-deceptive illusions. Superior human mentality merely permits the picaro to become a better animal, not to transcend his animality.

The metaphysics of the picaresque world is relativistic and fluid. Simplicius early perceives that "nothing in the world is more constant than inconstancy" (84). Uncertainty and continuous change are not, however, oppressive to the picaro, for he does not expect or admire permanence. Change means that the world consists of endlessly varied opportunities for new roles to be played and new advantages to be gained. Change may of course work to the picaro's disadvantage, as when Simplicius is transformed by smallpox from a handsome courtier admired by all the ladies to a pock-marked pariah, "so ugly that dogs would pee on me" (153). Neither condition is assumed to be definitive of his destiny or identity; each is merely one more condition that must be explored for its potential. Simplicius simply accepts his ugliness and learns to make his way by begging and fraud rather than by the seduction of wealthy ladies. Picaresque behavior is governed by an internalized acceptance of universal flux as the basic nature of the world. The picaro's philosophy is thus "to go with the times and make use of the inevitable" (215).

War is so often the setting for picaresque novels because its conditions intensify the problems to which the picaro must always adapt himself: rapid change, social disorder, irrationality, and constant threat of injury or death. War merely exaggerates normal social conditions. It matters little whether it is the Thirty Years' War or World War II, for in either case the personal problems of the picaro are the same. Joseph Heller's modern picaro, Yossarian, faces the same challenge as his counterpart Simplicius three centuries earlier: "It was all a sensible young gentleman like himself could do to maintain his perspective amid so much madness. And it was urgent that he did, for he knew his life was in danger."[15]

Yossarian struggles for survival in a world of aerial bombing rather than cavalry charges, but this merely means that his strategy must be more complex and quicker than that of Simplicius. Its principles are the same. Yossarian rejects the heroics expected of him in his role as a bombardier, preferring to survive as a coward: "He had decided to live forever or die in the attempt, and his only mission each time he went up was to come down alive" (30). He becomes a consummate master of the art of "evasive action," the erratic maneuvering of an airplane to avoid antiaircraft fire. Evasive action becomes a way of life for Yossarian whether on a bombing mission or on the ground, for threats are everywhere: "The enemy . . . is anybody who's going to get you killed, no matter *which* side he's on" (24). The American generals who plan bombing missions are as great a threat to his welfare as the German gunners who try to shoot him down. Questions of right and wrong, good and evil, friends and enemies dissolve into irrelevancy before the demanding task of survival in a world at war.

Evasive action means that Yossarian chooses to avoid danger rather than to destroy its source. In the picaresque manner, he assumes the state of his world to be a given condition that is beyond his power to improve. He accepts the irrational rules of war even when they change with every mission, and he tries to survive within them. He lives from minute to minute, limiting his vision of the world to the cockpit or whorehouse or briefing room, each with its own threat to his welfare and challenge to his ingenuity. Whatever the threat, he must adapt himself to its conditions with no hope of achieving peace and no idealistic delusions about his own capacity to triumph over adversity.

Ironically, Yossarian's evasions and fears are taken to be signs of his *failure* to adapt to the traditions of his culture. "You've been unable to adjust to the idea of war," his psychiatrist tells him. Yossarian agrees, then listens to a further exposition of the kind of adaptation that his society expects of him:

"You have a morbid aversion to dying. You probably resent the fact that you're at war and might get your head blown off any second."

"I more than resent it, sir. I'm absolutely incensed."

"You have deep-seated survival anxieties. And you don't like bigots, bullies, snobs, or hypocrites. Subconsciously there are many people you hate."

"Consciously, sir, consciously," Yossarian corrected in an effort to help. "I hate them consciously."

"You're antagonistic to the idea of being robbed, exploited, degraded, humiliated, or deceived. Misery depresses you. Ignorance depresses you. Persecution depresses you. Violence depresses you. Slums depress you. Greed depresses you. Crime depresses you. Corruption depresses you. You know, it wouldn't surprise me if you're a manic-depressive!"

"Yes, sir. Perhaps I am."

"Don't try to deny it."

"I'm not denying it, sir," said Yossarian, pleased with the miraculous rapport that finally existed between them. "I agree with all you've said."

"Then you admit you're crazy, do you?"

"Crazy?" Yossarian was shocked. "What are you talking about? Why am I crazy? You're the one who's crazy!" (312)

Picaresque sanity is recognition of the world's madness, not approval or emulation of it. The picaro cannot join forces with the agents of disaster and misery, for he does not share their ideologies, but neither does he seek to destroy them. Rather than hating the source of evil, he has compassion for its victims, among whom he numbers himself. He is thus out of step with the dominant power structure, in relation to which his actions seem insane. The picaro is a rogue partly because he refuses to endorse the ideologies of his time or their destructive consequences.

Yossarian is a responsible man, but not to the abstract values to which his corrupt society professes allegiance. Dignity, honor, morality, and patriotism are to the picaro the empty words behind which people hide their greed, vice, and treachery. Yossarian in the end runs away from the war and its pretenses of heroic nobility, choosing instead to save his own life and to help another victim of violence, the kid sister of a Roman whore. When he is condemned as an escapist for evading his patriotic duties, Yossarian insists: "I'm not running *away* from my responsibilities, I'm running *to* them. There's nothing negative about running away to save my life. You know who the escapists are, don't you?" (461). The escapists, of course, are the people who lie to themselves about human perfectibility, the righteousness of warfare, the importance of their own egos, and the sanctity of conventional morality.

The picaresque evasion of pain is radically different from the pastoral retreat in search of peace. Picaresque peace is merely a temporary avoidance of danger, never the permanent security sought in pastoral literature. As Yossarian prepares to desert from the army at the end of *Catch-22*, his friends caution him that "no one will ever be on your side, and you'll always live in danger of betrayal." "I live that way now," replies Yossarian (463). His future will be as dangerous as his past, but more on his own terms and with a better likelihood of survival than can be found within the war. Yossarian's life henceforth will be a calculated risk. When last seen, he is still running to avoid death.

Such inconclusive conclusions are typical of picaresque novels. The world's problems are never solved, no enemies are defeated, no new truth is realized, no peace is attained. In the course of the picaro's career he has gained only greater competence at survival, acceptance of responsibility for his own life, and a clearer understanding of the many threats surrounding him.

Picaresque Artistry

Picaresque action is not always defensive, but sometimes becomes highly creative. The wit necessary to save the picaro's life in time of war is applicable to the creation of beauty in times of relative peace. As a master manipulator and creator of illusions, the picaro has much in common with the artist, a conjunction that is explored by the twentieth-century German novelist Thomas Mann in his picaresque novel, *Confessions of Felix Krull, Confidence Man*.

As a young man, Felix Krull ponders the implications of various available perspectives upon the world. Great heroes and empire builders, he reasons, must see the world as a small place, like a chessboard upon which they expect to win their identity by managing the various pieces. The world of saints and hermits must also be a small and insignificant place from which it is best to withdraw in the hope of discovering a better one through mental fantasy or religious transcendence. Krull prefers to see the world as "a great and infinitely enticing phenomenon, offering priceless satisfactions and worthy in the highest degree of all my efforts and solicitude."[16] The vastness and complexity of the world is for Krull an endless source of opportunity for exploring his own potentials and talents. His motive is neither mastery of the world nor escape from its conditions, but the full utilization of his own talents to create a life rivaling the world itself in variety and excellence.

"He who really loves the world shapes himself to please it" is Krull's motto (65), and this defines his strategy as a member of society and as an artist. Adaptation to the given conditions of reality becomes more than the defensive technique of wartime picaros, for Krull regards himself as material to be shaped according to the potential richness and beauty of his circumstances. It is not the world that must be made to suit human pleasures, but humans to suit the world's. This does not just mean meeting the expectations of others, for Krull's conception of the world is not bounded by his contemporary society but includes the total context of natural and human history. The world he seeks to please includes both humanity and nature.

In order to please this larger world, it is often necessary to disappoint the expectations of contemporary society. Krull bends and breaks the conventions of his social context when they prevent him from exploiting his potential for creative experimentation. His idea of aristocracy, for instance, is based upon the observation that nature provides a graded hierarchy of beings according to innate gifts of talent and beauty. He early perceives that nature has endowed him with both: "I could not conceal from myself that I was made of superior stuff" (11). Yet his modest social position does not conform to his natural gifts, for society grades its members according to the artificial criteria of wealth and family, both of which are accidental. In order to bring his social position into agreement with his innate superiority, therefore, he must acquire money and rank by means of theft and deception.

There is no rancor or greed involved in these acts, and Krull takes pains to be sure that no one is hurt by them. His technique is to make himself so pleasing and attractive to others that they are moved to give him favors and gifts; while he profits, others feel no loss but give to him willingly. His fortune is acquired from a wealthy woman, slightly perverse, who gets a sexual thrill from being robbed of her jewels by a handsome young man like Krull, and his aristocratic rank is bestowed upon him by a profligate marquis whose identity Krull takes over in order to leave the young nobleman free to pursue anonymously his love affair with an actress. In spite of his unfortunately obscure birth, Krull thus earns the social credentials of superiority that correspond to his innate excellence.

When Krull finds social standards to be false, he corrects them—not for everyone, for that would produce equal falsity—but for himself. Krull is consistent with the picaresque code in his acceptance of the given social order, and in his belief that rank and order are natural hierarchical systems, not false social conventions. He rejects, for instance, the notion that nudity is democratic in that it abolishes the social ranks established by clothing styles. On the contrary, he argues, "Nakedness can only be called just in so far as it proclaims the naturally unjust constitution of the human race, unjust in that it is aristocratic" (90). Clothing displays false social status; its absence abolishes only the falsity and proclaims the natural rank order based upon beauty and agility of body.

The picaro is never a rebel against society, but merely a manipulator of its conditions for his own welfare in accordance with the principles of nature. When asked if he is a socialist, Krull answers, "No, indeed! . . . I find society enchanting just as it is and am on fire to earn its good opinion" (90). Of course he earns society's admiration by deception and illusion, thus earning the title "rogue," but his deceptions resemble those of art more than those of crime. He is an actor portraying the roles appropriate to his immediate context: "I seemed not only able to put on whatever social rank or personal characteristics I chose, but could actually adapt myself to any given period or century" (22). His social roles as elevator boy, waiter, pimp, and nobleman are played in order to fulfill the potential inherent in each role, not only to serve Krull's personal needs. He is a professional illusionist glorying in his adaptive skill.

Yet for all his admiration of society, his life remains by choice alone and isolated. Isolation is a necessary condition of picaresque action that emphasizes the dependence of the picaro upon his own devices. And it is not a cause for sorrow, as it is for the pastoral hero, but rather an opportunity. The picaro takes pride in his independence, even though it requires some sacrifice of personal intimacy. Krull accepts the fact that "close associations, friendship, and companionship were not to be my lot, but that I should instead be inescapably compelled to follow my strange path alone, dependent entirely upon myself, rigorously self-sufficient" (106). Although he remains on a congenial footing with those around him and even proves to be a master lover with women, Krull never permits intimacy to progress to the point of a dependency that might restrict his freedom to respond to new threats or opportunities.

Picaresque life is animal existence augmented by the imaginative and adaptive powers of the human mind. Unlike the pastoral mode, in which the mind is used to create alternatives to a dangerous present reality, the picaresque mode expresses acceptance of the present and adaptation to its conditions without concern for abstract ideologies or sentimental moralities. The comparison of the hero to animals, an almost universal feature of picaresque fiction, emphasizes the picaro's acceptance of biological limitations that define the nature of life and suggest the proper purposes that should govern the human use of intellect. Faulkner's rats and mules, Grimmelshausen's calf and goose, and the many other animals that recur in picaresque literary art are most often used as models of appropriate action rather than as images of debased life that threaten some conventional standard of human dignity.

The final chapters of Mann's *Felix Krull* are devoted to the hero's exploration of his own relationship to animal and biological existence as he is conducted through the Lisbon Museum of Natural History by its director. The first animal Krull sees inside the museum is a magnificent white stag mounted against a forest background. He enjoys the likeness between himself and the stag, not only because both are well-formed and beautiful, but also because of their common attitude toward their environments. Stag and Krull are "dignified and alert . . . calm yet wary," and ready to "disappear at a bound into the darkness" at the slightest sign of danger (298). The stag is a handsome picaro, adept at evasive action like his human counterpart Felix Krull.

The record of evolution displayed in the museum further shows Krull his kinship with the animals as well as his separation from them. He sees "the contrast between my own fineness and elegance and the primitive crudity of many of the uncanny-looking fossils, the primitive crustaceans, cephalopods, brachiopods, tremendously ancient sponges and entrail-less lily-stars.' . . . These first beginnings, however absurd and lacking in dignity and usefulness, were preliminary moves in the direction of me—that is, of Man" (301). Higher evolutionary forms, mammals and primates, further confirm Krull's joy at his newfound unity with all animal life: "In the end they all prefigured me, even though disguised as in some sorry jest" (304).

When his tour brings him to the displays of early humans, his pleasure in evolutionary continuity is further confirmed, for in primitive people he sees "what had been striving toward me from the grey reaches of antiquity" (304). He is confirmed in the perception that he had earlier derived from his conversations with the museum director: "Men are descended from animals in just about the same way that the organic is descended from the inorganic. Something was added" (271). Consciousness was added, the gift that augments the process of evolution but does not separate humanity from that process.

Consciousness permits people to enjoy their animal powers and beauties more than the other animals can. As Krull sees it, people do by will only what other animals do by instinct, and so people become responsible for what they are. Unattractive animals cannot be blamed for their ugliness, but among people it is "culpable to be ugly." Krull finds ugliness "a kind of carelessness" that offends him and that contrasts sharply with his own artistic attitude toward himself: "Out of innate consideration for the world that was awaiting me, I took care while I was being formed that I should not offend its eyes. . . . I'd call it a kind of self-discipline" (317). Krull has here restated the law of creative picaresque behavior with which his career began: "He who really loves the world shapes himself to please it."

Consciousness, intelligence, language, imagination—these are to the picaro the means for artistic adaptation to his environment. He uses his gifts for self-defense, but also for playing with others and with his surroundings. Dominance over his environment is not a goal, nor does he use imaginative powers for the creation of idealistic fantasies. Accepting the accidents of natural and social history that have produced him and the environment that defines his possibilities, the picaro applies his intelligence toward making the best of whatever the world may offer.

Rogues and Saints

The roots of pastoral and picaresque go deeply into Western cultural traditions, the collective psyche, and perhaps into human evolutionary origins. It is not easy to tell whether the two modes reflect differences in human temperament and personality or are expressions of beliefs that people hold. The pastoral mode looks something like an ideology, for pastoral writers often claim to know how people should live and expect them to mend their ways; they often assume life to be perfectible, however great their despair at discovering that people often reject their chances for perfection. The picaresque, on the other hand, is more descriptive than prescriptive. Picaresque stories are not much help in the search for what ought to be because they are concerned only with what is. They offer a mirror of behavior, not a model for imitation.

The pastoral hero is born an aristocrat, socially superior to others and highly sophisticated. His anthropocentric world exists for the purpose of perfecting human welfare and elevating the human spirit. Confident that he is at the center of creation, he yet sees the failure of his fellow humans to achieve their potential and he is oppressed by this discovery. He regretfully turns away from his society and its unnecessary miseries, accepts his isolation as a painful consequence, and looks for renewal from an agricultural version of nature. Nature, he hopes, will renew human nobility through her pastoral hero.

The picaro begins life with no credentials of dignity or status. Neither his social status nor his metaphysics supports a claim to superiority over anything. His main concern is with survival. He quickly learns that survival is a tricky process requiring that he attend closely to his immediate environment for both threats and opportunities. Since the world has no plans for him, he is free to become whatever seems appropriate or interesting. He lives as an intelligent animal, interested in the present, and ready to play when the opportunity arises.

Morality is a cornerstone of pastoral life. People are assumed to be naturally good, and if they nevertheless seem corrupt, it must be because the institutions of civilization have made them so. The experience of nature is seen as therapeutic, restoring people to the natural goodness with which they began. Pastoral literature loves noble savages, and urges people to regain the purity that has been sacrificed to civilization.

The picaresque vision usually discovers early that exalted moral postures can quickly lead to someone's death or undoing. Morality is often dangerous to the picaro, either because it limits his flexibility, or because he runs the risk of suffering from the rigidities of others. The picaro is skeptical of moral abstractions, and he rarely thinks about good or evil. If survival is a moral principle, he is enthusiastically in favor of it.

Pastoral emotions tend toward the melodramatic. Self-pity is a common beginning for a pastoral narrative. The hero is despondent because the world has not treated him as well as he deserves. He finds solace in nostalgic fantasies about the good old days of his own youth or of humanity's in the Garden of Eden. His belief that life has been beautiful inspires him with hope that it can be good again if only he can restore the proper conditions. The pastoral quest is a sentimental journey away from present pain in search of past peace. It is never a successful quest. The emotional cycle of pastoral experience normally moves from nostalgia to hope, to disillusionment, to final despair.

Compassion for suffering may be the most serious emotion experienced by picaresque heroes. The picaro makes little distinction between his own misfortune and that of others, treating both with solicitude and resignation. He sees pain as the consequence of his own errors rather than evidence of the world's malice, so he is more likely to be self-mocking than self-pitying. He more often laughs at the world's absurdities than cries over its inequities. As he has no hope, he need never suffer despair. His career does not proceed in a cycle, but is merely an ongoing account of his increasingly adept durability as he responds to a series of surprises. Picaresque narratives do not reach neat conclusions and their heroes never achieve either fulfillment or discovery, for the picaresque mode presents life as a continuous process, perhaps meaningless but compellingly interesting.

Pastoral life is polarized, presenting mutually exclusive alternatives between which a choice must be made. The good must be achieved, the evil rooted out; peace is excellent, war is hell; elegant simplicity is preferable to fearful complexity; purity is our goal, pollution our punishment; society is corrupt but nature is sinless. Pastoral motivation is always in the direction of positive goals that are believed to be attainable if only their opposites can be avoided. The pastoral world is a battleground between God and Satan, and the pastoral hero is enlisted among the angels. He is, to be sure, a rear-echelon angel not involved in the battle itself, but he prays fervently for God's side to win.

The picaro does not positively search for peace but merely hopes to avoid war. He is rarely able to distinguish between good and evil except in their most basic forms, pleasure and pain—and even these are often mixed. His world is systemic rather than polar. Many gods, many Satans, and many beings of indeterminate moral status contend before his eyes, all holding both threats and promises. He does not expect the world to meet his conditions, but he will do all he can to meet its. His constant motivation is to blend into the system where he finds himself.

Images of environment and metaphors of behavior reflect the separate value systems of the pastoral and the picaresque. Garden and farm are the dominant figures in the pastoral mode, while wilderness and the city are the basic images of the picaresque. These images have carried far beyond their literary origins and have become influential habits of the modern mind.

Botany dominates the pastoral scene. Plants symbolize the kind of life most desired by pastoral seekers: rooted, placid, beautiful. The only animals admitted to pastoral landscapes are those domestic creatures whose behavior is similarly calm; nervous and aggressive animals are fenced out. The pastoral psyche yearns for the peace of vegetative life. The typical stages of pastoral narrative begin with the desire to retreat to a simpler life, followed by recognition of helplessness before the world's cruelty, and ending in sad resignation or despair. The attempt to achieve the values of the garden—nourishment, beauty, peacefulness, stability—leads inevitably to disappointment in a perverse and competitive world.

The picaresque wilderness, of course, leads to no great goals either, but since the picaro has no expectations he can hardly be disappointed about that. Picaresque literature does not express the kind of hopelessness implied by tragedy or existential despair, for these traditions seem to hold the world responsible for being reasonable and just to humans and regard its failures as somehow an affront to humanity. The picaro is hopeless only in the sense that he sees hope to be an irrelevant concept, an unjustifiable expectation of the future that offers no help in dealing with present problems. The picaro's only "hope" is that he may succeed at the day-to-day business of keeping himself alive; if a wolf can be said to hope for a meal each day and the avoidance of trappers who want his pelt, then the picaro can be said to hope. In the picaresque tradition, people are shown living as other animals live, confronting the present defensively and opportunistically, without expectations or illusions, proud of strength but accurately aware of limitations, mistrustful but not cynical or malicious, and above all adaptive to the immediate environment.

Perhaps the major difference between pastoral and picaresque lies in the application each makes of human intelligence. The pastoral intellect uses the rational capacity of the mind to criticize the inadequacies of present experience and its imaginative talents to create alternatives to the present. It is characterized by abstract ideas—truth, justice, goodness, love—intended to lead toward a fulfillment of human potential at some future time. The picaresque intellect instead concentrates upon the study of immediate reality, and its imagination upon the creation of strategies for survival. Picaresque liberty is not escape from misfortune, but confidence in one's ability to persist in spite of it.

Modern cities, like ancient Rome, are messy, expensive, chaotic, and dangerous. Those who flee them in search of rural peace and quiet are following a pastoral way that Western culture has endorsed since Virgil. The pastoral tradition also makes it plain that this quest is likely to fail, for the seeker of peace and simplicity is likely to carry inner conflict and anger, and these will govern his or her life more than the rural environment will. Escape into fantasies is not a workable solution to urban and existential ills.

What the picaresque tradition lacks in dignity and respectability, it makes up for in clear-eyed practicality. In the picaresque eye, cities and wild places are all full of both danger and opportunity, and wherever one finds oneself is the place where life must be lived as well as possible. Picaresque life is infinite play, with no hope of winning much, but endless enthusiasm for keeping the play alive.

6 * New Stories

Helen and I live on a forested Island in Puget Sound near Seattle. On our property I have made a trail through the forest where we walk, meditate, study, and teach the forest ecology around us. Every autumn comes the time of the spiders, when we can scarcely walk the trail without breaking many webs strung across the five-foot-wide trail. I've found that I can pass in one direction, catching many webs on my face, then turn and walk in the opposite direction fifteen minutes later to find new webs in the same places I just disturbed. How does a little spider bridge a gap that is several hundred times its own body length in just a few minutes?

The answer came from ethologist Karl von Frisch, whose book *Animal Architecture* describes how spiders spin a tiny kite that they then fly on the breeze with a silken thread until it adheres to another object, providing the first strand in what will become an elaborate and beautiful orb web, a place where the spider will live and earn her living.[1] It is a complex task that no one has taught the spider how to do, for spiders are all orphans who grow up without parental supervision or cultural learning. If a spider is not born knowing what it needs to survive, there is no support system to help it.

Spiders are picaros, dependent only upon themselves for their needs and for their survival.

A major discovery of our time is that people are more like spiders than we have suspected. Steven Pinker, the linguist who has extended the linguistic revolution begun by Noam Chomsky in the 1950s, asserts that "people know how to talk in more or less the sense that spiders know how to spin webs . . . spiders spin spider webs because they have spider brains, which give them the urge to spin and the competence to succeed."[2] Spiders spin *by instinct*, and people use language *by instinct*, an assertion that would have seemed intellectual heresy a few decades ago, when language was commonly used as the main criterion for separating humans from all other creatures, and was considered our species' crowning invention and the center of the unique human cultural tradition. Language is no less miraculous than it has always been, but it is now possible to think about it in the context of evolutionary history.

The New Stories that are now emerging are stories that connect humans in evolutionary time, in ecological and cosmic space, and across cultural and species boundaries. The features that we share with other times, places, and forms of life have become more significant than the differences separating us from them. There is a Universal Grammar at the foundation of all languages, just as there is a universal need for play in all birds and mammals, and a comic story to be lived by all species in their strategy for survival. The most promising stories for our time are those that connect us in complex and systemic ways to the basic principles of life.

This Story's Story

This book has walked several steps along the pathway toward a New Story. It began in my vague realization sometime during the 1960s that language and literature were features of human natural history and behavior, and that they probably played roles in the processes of natural selection and human survival. A proposal to explore the possibilities of these ideas was supported by the National Endowment for the Humanities in 1971–72, permitting me to do the research for the first edition of this book. I wanted to explore the linkages connecting literature, philosophy, and ecology, and I sought help from some of the most provocative thinkers I could find.

One of my mentors was Dr. Konrad Lorenz, who invited me to visit him at the Max Planck Institute in southern Germany where he and his colleagues were pursuing comparative studies in animal and human behavior. Later, in 1973, Lorenz was to share with Karl von Frisch and Nikolaas Tinbergen the Nobel Prize in Physiology or Medicine for their joint creation of the science of ethology, the study of animal behavior. I lived with Lorenz for several weeks, going with him daily into the field where he was studying his resident flock of greylag geese. He explained the behaviors we were seeing in the geese—aggression, pair bonding, mating, parenting, rank order, and so on—as a complex combination of inherited instinct and environmental learning. From Lorenz, and from the dozens of other researchers who were working around him, I began to see that human behavior was a product of the same evolutionary and environmental forces that were at work in the lives of other animals. I was on my way.

From Germany, I went to Geneva at the invitation of Dr. Eugene Carson Blake, director of the World Council of Churches, who had been a family friend for years. Dr. Blake invited me to sit in on several major religious policy discussions. It was at a time, shortly after the first Earth Day, when several scholars had laid the blame for ecological disaster heavily on the shoulders of Christianity, claiming that the Earth had been devalued by the Christian tradition in favor of otherworldly perspectives. I heard church leaders from several Christian denominations defending their tradition, and, for the first time, trying to describe what roles religion might play in protecting natural environments and restoring ecological health. One consensus was reached, agreeing that Christians should refer less to "dominion" over nature and should instead emphasize "stewardship" over nature. Some Christian groups have not come much further than that since the 1970s.

I visited the University of Oslo, where I had heard that the world's first program in Ecophilosophy had recently been founded. That visit was the beginning of a long friendship with Dr. Arne Naess, originator of studies in Ecophilosophy. Arne and others at the University of Oslo joined me in my search for links between the humanities and the biological sciences, and we are still active in that quest. It was about this time that Arne Naess published a paper that introduced the term "deep ecology" to refer to philosophical and cultural thinking about natural environments. Deep ecology was to become one of the major developments in environmental thinking over the next two decades.

I also visited Sir Frank Fraser Darling, a well-known English ecologist whom I had met in Alaska. Sir Frank was a widely published field ecologist and a leading British conservationist. As a guest at his country home, I learned about the integration of ecology and aesthetics, for Sir Frank was a knowledgeable collector of indigenous arts from many parts of the world, and he spoke of the many ways in which art expresses the relationships between people and the land, plants, and animals that share their part of the world. Sir Frank was one of the first ecologists to describe animal play in detail in his 1937 book, *A Herd of Red Deer*.[3]

My friendship with Paul Shepard also began at this time, and continued until his death in 1996. Paul's life work has been to explore the rich ways in which human life and natural systems interpenetrate one another, and the sad consequences that follow when those interconnections are broken or blocked. Paul brought together biological science, philosophy, anthropology, psychology, and aesthetics in a series of books that have studied ancient hunting and gathering cultures, childhood, the roles of animals in human mentality, and the implications of ecology for enriching personal and cultural life.

I mention these personal connections not so much to acknowledge their help to me (though I am deeply grateful for it), but to establish the intellectual context of the early 1970s so that we can better assess what has happened since then. It is significant, I think, that those people were all exploring the beginnings of themes that have been developed and embellished since then. Much that seemed revolutionary then has come to be ordinary now, and some of the astonishing new developments of our time have actually grown gradually over the past few decades. Our new story appears to have an integrity of its own.

Evolutionary Psychology

When *The Comedy of Survival* first appeared in 1974,[4] some people were shocked and angry at comparisons between animals and literary characters, or at the idea that something so undignified and trivial as comedy could be presented as a philosophy of life. Some of the same people, I imagine, were even more angry one year later when E. O. Wilson published *Sociobiology*, a comprehensive study of the evolutionary basis for animal and human behavior.[5] This book touched off the great "sociobiology debate" that lasted a decade or so. A central issue in that discussion was whether humans can exercise free will or have their behavior determined by genetic inheritance. A greater shock was delivered in 1976 when Richard Dawkins argued in *The Selfish Gene* that the unit of natural selection is the gene, not the organism.[6] What happens to human dignity and freedom of choice when all significant decisions are made by mindless genes?

In very different ways, these books challenged the humanistic beliefs that Western people have held about themselves for the past century. They have generally assumed that animal behavior is rigidly controlled by biology, while human behavior rests upon freedom of choice within the constraints of human-created culture. They have assumed that individual humans are born as small blank slates waiting for parents and culture to write upon them and give them language, values, and proper behavior. These premises have guided academic inquiry into the human condition, and have been the basis for most educational policies, social and political programs, and public values. If evolution and genes were really the governing forces behind human behavior, we would have to rethink most of our ideas about ourselves.

That is the exciting work that is happening now. Rarely does the word "sociobiology" appear these days, for too many academic toes were mashed in the frenzy of that debate, but there is a growing literature that is sometimes called "evolutionary psychology." The task of unraveling the genetic and instinctual components of behavior is proceeding on many fronts. Much of that research is summarized in science writer Robert Wright's book *The Moral Animal*.[7] Wright finds that contemporary Darwinian thinking has rediscovered the idea of human nature, seeing "the world's undeniably diverse cultures as products of a single human nature responding to widely varying circumstances."[8] Just as human anatomy is universally the same with only minor adaptations to local environments, so the human mind is endowed by evolutionary history with a psychic unity.

Wright describes the relationship between heredity and environment as a system of "knobs and tunings." The knobs are those characteristics that are universal in all human cultures, such as feelings of guilt and the need for social approval. The tunings are the ways in which the knobs are turned by particular cultural or environmental influences, indicating how guilt is to be expressed, or providing rituals of social approval. Human nature, according to the recent research in evolutionary psychology, has knobs for almost all aspects of human behavior, and the knobs are instinctual patterns deeply rooted in evolutionary history beyond the reach of cultures to change in any significant way.

The new Darwinian perspectives that Wright describes "touch on just about everything that matters: romance, love, sex . . . friendship and enmity . . . selfishness, self-sacrifice, guilt . . . social status and social climbing . . . the differing inclinations of men and women in areas such as friendship and ambition . . . racism, xenophobia, war . . . deception, self-deception, and the unconscious mind . . . various psychopathologies . . . the love-hate relationship between siblings . . . the tremendous capacity of parents to inflict psychic damage on their children, and so on."[9] As Wright unfolds the story of all these topics, the theme of the selfish gene emerges as the guiding force in human behavior. The strategies developed during millions of years of evolutionary history appear to be focused upon replicating genes from one generation to the next, and human behavior emerges as little more than a device to assure that outcome.

"It's safe to call this a cynical view of behavior," Wright acknowledges. "There's nothing new about cynicism. Indeed, some would call it the story of our time."[10] Cynicism undercuts concepts like beauty, nobility, love, and friendship, seeing them as nothing but the product of genes blindly replicating themselves while masquerading as noble sentiments and high moral philosophy. It is true that ideas about human freedom of choice and nobility are hard to maintain in the face of evidence from evolutionary psychology, but those have begun to seem like fossils of the Enlightenment anyway, retained only in the vocabularies of antique academics and stuffy politicians. Yet it is hard to follow Wright on his path of cynicism.

I looked carefully in Wright's book for some information about play behavior. Strangely, there is no mention of play anywhere in the book, and no index listing for the subject. Yet play is an instinctive pattern of behavior shared by birds and mammals over many millions of years. There is a large scientific literature on play in ethology, psychology, anthropology, and evolutionary biology. Play's literary manifestation, comedy, is also an ancient pattern of behavior with a large body of knowledge attached to it. For whatever reason this important category of human and animal behavior was ignored by Wright, his cynicism is a consequence of the omission. It is not possible to consider play without finding joy, spontaneity, cooperation, and the makings of love.

The discovery that genes are busily using me to replicate themselves does not depress me, lead me into cynicism, or persuade me to devalue human history or my own life. Rather, I am inclined to think of those genes as playing together, with me as their playground. It may be a purposeless game that we are all involved in, but it is endlessly fascinating, and it is an infinite game.

Richard Dawkins comes closer to a comic view of evolution in *River out of Eden: A Darwinian View of Life*.[11] Dawkins offers scores of examples of complex behaviors and anatomical features, including detailed descriptions of the stages of evolutionary development for intricate organs like the human eye or elaborate behaviors such as the waggle-dances by which bees communicate to one another the distance and direction of food sources. He describes the process as "doing good by stealth."[12] Stealth here appears as a necessary component of a gradual creative process, not as an attempt to deceive creatures into performing against their will. The "good" that is created by stealth is more life, and that sounds to me like a playful process.

Innate Language

One of Paul Shepard's books, *Thinking Animals*,[13] was, like many of Paul's books, so far ahead of its time that its audience was unable to understand it, and the book languished. One of its central ideas was that the human brain has developed its main features in response to the need for naming and knowing the animals and plants of the ancestral human environment. Enough water has now gone under our intellectual bridges so that the innate features of the human mind can be considered anew, as linguist Steven Pinker has done in *The Language Instinct*.[14] Pinker marshals comprehensive evidence to show that human language is based upon a Universal Grammar common to all languages, and that this structure is an instinctual feature inherited from millions of years of evolutionary history. As Paul Shepard said, we have been thinking animals for a long time.

Pinker's argument adds strength to the growing idea that there is a human nature that comes into the world well equipped for life with the mental software needed to learn the lessons that culture and society have to teach.

Pinker's news is that "complexity in the mind is not caused by learning; learning is caused by complexity in the mind."[15] Avoiding the worn-out arguments about "nature versus nurture" or "heredity versus environment," Pinker proposes instead a structure he calls The Integrated Causal Model, an approach that "seeks to explain how evolution caused the emergence of a brain, which causes psychological processes like knowing and learning, which cause the acquisition of the values and knowledge that make up a person's culture."[16] This integrated approach, with language at its core, is a meeting ground for the natural and social sciences, and, I would add, for literature and ecology.

Steven Pinker does not limit his interests to language, but considers other innate behaviors that seem to be a universal part of the human heritage. He draws upon the work of Donald E. Brown, an anthropologist who, following Chomsky's work on Universal Grammar, tried to describe the Universal heritage of all people in his book *Human Universals*.[17] He reproduces Brown's list of characteristics found in all cultures at all times, a list requiring three tightly packed pages of print. I will reproduce a few samples to give the flavor of these universals:

> Value placed on articulateness. Gossip. Lying. Misleading. Verbal humor. . . . Nonlinguistic vocal communications such as cries and squeals. Interpreting intention from behavior. Recognized facial expressions of happiness, sadness, anger, fear, surprise, disgust, and contempt. . . . Sense of self versus other, responsibility, voluntary versus involuntary behavior, intention, private inner life, normal versus abnormal mental states. . . . Manufacture of, and dependence upon many kinds of tools, many of them permanent, made according to culturally transmitted motifs, including cutters, pounders, containers, string, levers, spears. . . . A standard pattern and time for weaning. Living in groups, which claim a territory and have a sense of being a distinct people. . . . Status and prestige, both assigned (by kinship, age, sex) and achieved. Some degree of economic inequality. Division of labor by sex and age. . . . Etiquette. Hospitality. Feasting. Diurnality. Standards of sexual modesty. Sex generally in private. Fondness for sweets.[18]

Pinker is quick to point out that this is not a list of instincts; it is, however, "a list of complex interactions between a universal human nature and the conditions of living in a human body on this planet,"[19] which sounds to me a lot like a list of instincts. I like the list, for it offers a sense of connectedness with all humans in all times and places that satisfies my need for communion in time and space.

It also astonishes me and depresses me, for nowhere on this list of human universals is play mentioned, although play is present in all cultures and all periods, and in all species with complex brains. By some amazing alchemy, comedy and play are cloaked with an invisibility that is rarely seen by the intellect, no matter how keen it may be to detect other subtleties. The great Edward O. Wilson was mentor to one of the most influential scholars of animal play, Robert Fagen, yet Wilson's book *On Human Nature* contains no reference to play, nor do his two volumes on *Biophilia*, although centered by definition on the love of life.[20] I suppose it may be just as well, for when great intellects do think about play, they often destroy its spontaneity and write dreary books about it. The scholarly literature on play tends to be glum and mechanical, and almost never playful. Yet I know in my heart and mind that play and comedy are somewhere near the center of what it means to be a free animal on this planet, that play connects our species to many other species, and that these things have been true for many millions of years. Comedy and play are important parts of the planet's Universal Language.

Animal Minds

Every autumn, the crows in my neighborhood harvest hazel nuts. Crows are perfectly capable of cracking the nuts for themselves, but they are also famous for finding clever ways to get what they want without working too hard. So my neighboring crows place their hazel nuts on the road and wait for a passing car to run over them, leaving the nut meats easily plucked from the pavement. Mythologies of many cultures have recognized the intelligence of crows and ravens, and have credited them with special powers. I find it natural enough to think of these crows as intelligent creatures who are solving a problem in a practical and sensible way, just as you or I might. But for the past few centuries, academic people have been in the habit of explaining such behavior as the result of automatic responses or mechanical reactions to environmental stimuli. Behaviorism has until recently been an unassailable premise of most psychological and ethological research into animal and human behavior. That citadel is no longer impregnable.

The new science of cognitive ethology explores the relationships between mentality and behavior in animals, as well as the possibilities for animal consciousness. One of the champions of this new field is Donald R. Griffin, author of several books and many articles on animal mentality and consciousness.[21] By taking great pains to address the assumptions of behaviorist interpretations of animal behavior, Griffin elaborates a powerful critique of the behaviorist approach. He also provides hundreds of examples of animals behaving intelligently—showing high versatility, appropriateness of behavior to unique situations, problem-solving ability, and spontaneous acts that are hard to account for either by genetic inheritance or environmental conditioning.

Many animals show intelligence and imagination in finding and manipulating food, inventing complex entrapments or avoidances as predators or prey, constructing intricate shelters or other artifacts, making and using tools, communicating with one another and across species lines, deceiving and manipulating one another, and generally displaying a broad range of behaviors that are very familiar to people, for they are parts of our repertoire as well. Griffin also considers evidence for the presence of concepts and beliefs in animal mentality, and speculates about the existence of animal fantasies and imagination, concluding that "animals may experience fantasies as well as realistic representations of their environments."[22] Part of his evidence for this comes from studies of rapid eye movement (REM) sleep in mammals, which has been shown to be associated with dreaming, just as it is in humans. Griffin concludes, "It would indeed be ironic if evidence that animals think consciously should come to be derived from an understanding of their dreams."[23] Considering the enormous importance of dreams for understanding human consciousness, it seems likely that the same route will open to us the minds of many of our fellow creatures.

Griffin, like many of the academics we have discussed, does not seem to consider animal play important in understanding animal behavior or mentality. I can only understand play's invisibility by guessing that something like dignity is very important to most scholars, and that play has a reputation for being undignified and childlike. (Part of the task of this book is to make a case for the value of scholarship that is sometimes undignified and childlike.)

There is a slim but provocative connection between REM sleep and play behavior that may prove to be significant. Psychiatrist Stuart Brown tells me of his research into the amounts of play needed in the normal day of an animal. It turns out that for a dozen or so species of mammals, there is a "recommended daily dose" of play of about one to two hours per day. When these figures are compared with the amounts of REM sleep needed by the same species of mammals, they turn out to be almost identical. No one is quite sure what functions REM sleep performs, but there is general agreement that deprivation of REM sleep causes abnormal mental and physical states. If the mystery of REM sleep is unraveled, it may turn out to be connected with the impulse to play. It is tempting to guess that play may perform some subtle regulatory function during waking hours that is like the function performed by REM sleep at night.[24]

Another thing that may prevent scientists and scholars from paying close attention to animal consciousness and to play may be the fear of "anthropomorphism," the intellectual sin of attributing human qualities to nonhuman animals. Poets and storytellers have been freely crossing the boundaries among species for many thousands of years, but sometime in the eighteenth century it was decided that such looseness was incompatible with intellectual rigor. Now even that shibboleth is falling, thanks to books like Theodore Xenophon Barber's *The Human Nature of Birds*.[25] Barber collects and summarizes the past few decades of research into avian intelligence, and finds that the evidence supports these conclusions:

1 Birds have many abilities that humans assume are unique to humans, including musical ability (appreciation, composition, and performance), ability to form abstract concepts, ability to use intelligence flexibly to cope with constantly changing life demands, and ability to play with joy and mate erotically.

2 Although humans are superior to birds in certain kinds of intelligence (such as symbolic-linguistic intelligence), birds are superior to humans in other kinds of intelligence (such as navigational intelligence).

3 Birds are not only intelligent, aware, and willful; they also can communicate meaningfully with humans and relate to them as close, caring friends.[26]

It is satisfying to note that the ability "to play with joy" is included, and indeed Barber gives appropriate significance to play in his explanations of bird behavior. Barber provides research reports, anecdotes, and personal observation in support of all of the above assertions, and presents a compelling case for bird intelligence. In his final chapters, he extends this logic to include consciousness for primates, cetaceans, fishes, and even ants. He describes the newfound awareness of animal consciousness as a "revolution in thought" and predicts its coming triumph: "In the long run the revolutionary anthropomorphic view of birds will become dominant because . . . it can be empirically demonstrated that birds have the characteristics that people thought were unique to people and as these demonstrations become increasingly more comprehensive and powerful, a new generation of scientists and laypeople will accept the essential human-avian similarity as a basic scientific truth."[27] Barber's vision includes a world where people and animals survive together in a cared-for environment, and where communication, cooperation, and play are the central activities. That sounds to me like a comic world.

Cosmic Comedy

Thomas Berry, philosopher and theologian, called for the emergence of a New Story in his 1988 book, *The Dream of the Earth*: "We need something that will supply in our times what was supplied formerly by our traditional religious story. If we are to achieve this purpose, we must begin where everything begins in human affairs—with the basic story, our narrative of how things came to be, how they came to be as they are, and how the future can be given some satisfying direction. We need a story that will educate us, a story that will heal, guide, and discipline us."[28] One year after that book appeared, a group of some thirty-five scholars and artists gathered at a conference center in California to begin the process of exploring a New Story for our time. None of us was arrogant enough to suppose that we could create a new mythology that would serve modern times the way the Christian story or the Progress story had formerly served. Rather, we began with the premise that *The Universe is a Story*, and that our task is to discover our own most appropriate and creative role to be played within that large tale.

Ingredients for a New Story are abundant. Quantum physics offers a detailed account of the origin of the universe in a gigantic explosive event that took place some fifteen billion years ago. Life on Earth began some four billion years ago with the first prokaryotic cells, and two billion years later the first eukaryotic cells appeared, bringing with them the capacity to use oxygen, to survive by consuming other life forms, and to reproduce sexually. Evolution was off and running then, and has since produced the huge diversity of life forms and ecosystems that provide the basis for a modern Story of Life. Science and scholarship have provided new ways to read and interpret that story with the development of systems theory, complex mathematics, and computational technology. People have also begun to change their perceptions of themselves and their interrelationships by redefining the meaning of social justice, cultural diversity, and gender relationships. Blending these rich ingredients into an integrated and coherent story is a central task of our time. When it happens, perhaps modern people will enjoy living as many traditional cultures have lived: knowing who we are, where we came from, and what matters. We will be oriented in space, time, and spirit.

Thomas Berry collaborated with physicist Brian Swimme to begin that task in their book, *The Universe Story*.[29] They propose that the New Story will develop as part of a new biological era on planet Earth that they call the Ecozoic, to succeed the previous eras, Paleozoic, Mesozoic, and Cenozoic. In the Ecozoic era, people will again perceive the Earth as a whole and themselves as responsible parts of a whole and integrated system: "This new story of an emergent universe, properly understood as having a psychic-spirit dimension from the beginning, is really an enhancement of all that humans have ever experienced previously in their perceptions of the universe. We now have the wonder, not merely that we are related to and intimate with everything about us, but that we have a cousin relationship with every being in the universe, especially with the living beings of the planet Earth."[30] A new perception like this will require the integration of modern scientific knowledge with emerging new understandings of planetary politics and economics, new interracial and intercultural cooperation, new visions of the relationships of the sexes, and a new sense of planetary justice that honors the rights of all creatures and the ecosystems they constitute.

That's a tall order, but there is evidence that human consciousness is capable of such an integration. Not lately, of course. For several hundred years our civilization has been preoccupied with separating itself from the natural world, exploiting it, and carving an anthropocentric monument to itself. But with the new knowledge of complex systems, and with a new terror growing from the awareness of our destructive capability, we may now be approaching a time when genuine integration of humanity and the cosmos is possible.

Conservationist David Brower, a mountaineer, often says that when one is lost, the best thing to do is to go back to the last place where you knew where you were, and start over. The last time Western culture was sufficiently oriented to tell an integrated story of humanity and the cosmos was before the rise of industry and technology, before the rise of science, before modern cities and economies were founded, and before the Renaissance with its humanistic divisions of knowledge into compartments. That takes us back about seven hundred years. The storyteller was Dante Alighieri, the place was Florence, and the story was a Comedy.

7 * Dante and the Comic Way

Dante Alighieri, the fourteenth-century Italian poet, called his great poem simply *The Comedy*. Theologians later mistook Dante's intentions and added *Divine* to the title. The mistake has since led readers to see the work as a textbook of medieval religious beliefs. But Dante said that his purpose was "to remove those living in this life from the state of misery and lead them to the state of felicity."[1] To accomplish this, Dante believed that he must present the world in all its complex multiplicity so that people could better understand where they were in relation to everything else, material and spiritual. Misery, according to Dante, is the result of mistaking or distorting one's vision so that only a fragment of reality can be seen, and then taking that fragment for the whole. Felicity becomes possible as the eye learns to see the millions of fragments that make up the universe interacting with one another to create a cosmos. Misery arises from simplified and narrow vision; felicity lies in participation in systemic complexity.

Dante's *Comedy*, like all truly great literature, describes concrete instances of human universals. Dante was writing about the particular people and events of fourteenth-century Florence, yet he does so in a way that illuminates human experiences that could as easily be found in fifth-century Peking or twentieth-century San Francisco. His cosmology is derived from Ptolemy and Thomas Aquinas, yet its essence and complexity are compatible with modern quantum theory and complex dynamic systems. Dante provides one of the rare instances of deep insight into the concrete realities of the present that reveals timeless and universal qualities. This poet from seven hundred years ago speaks in a modern voice, and will no doubt do so seven hundred years hence.

The view of life presented in the *Comedy* can be called ecological in the largest sense of the term. Dante's Hell is a sink of noxious gases, polluted water, and denuded forests. The people there have caused their own misery and have created the miserable environment in which they are trapped. They all suffer an impairment of vision that causes them to exaggerate their selfish rights and to satisfy themselves at any cost to others or to the world around them. Purgatory is a place of learning, where souls discover what else there is in the world beside themselves. As they increase in understanding and perspective, they begin to see the causes of misery and degradation, and so gradually become free of them. Paradise is an extremely complex place, physically and intellectually. The inhabitants see themselves as part of the intricate physical, spiritual, and social life of the world, and they are intensely aware of their own relationships to what they see. Paradise is where human awareness expands to comprehend and to participate in the complexity of things.

Fully as important as the human souls who inhabit Dante's three symbolic environments are the environments themselves. Hell, Purgatory, and Paradise are settings that correspond to the moral and psychological states of the people within them. Since all souls have chosen the particular circumstances that define their lives, they have helped create an environment that perfectly mirrors their values. In Dante's imaginative vision, human actions build their own most appropriate environment.

Inferno

Hell is an image of both moral and biological pollution. Its physical conditions are the environmental equivalent of moral error. The imagery is strikingly similar to that of the modern industrialized, overpopulated, polluted world. Hell is a familiar environment for anyone who feels at home in New York or Los Angeles.

Hell's air is clouded with contaminants and foul odors. The carnal sinners of the second circle whirl in a storm of "dark air."[2] Further down, Dante discovers that "his eye could hardly journey far / across the black air and heavy fog."[3] Everyone in Hell squints because of the stinging air that cannot pass enough light for clear vision. As Dante descends, the air pollution index rises until at the tenth level of Malebolge he is reminded of an ancient disaster at Aegina "when the air was so infected that / all animals, down to the little worm, / collapsed."[4] Cocytus, the frozen lake at Hell's greatest depth, is clouded by a "dense and darkened fog" that all but prevents both breathing and sight.[5]

Hell's waters never run pure. From a spring on the fifth circle the River Styx spurts forth its waters "even darker than deep purple,"[6] which Dante follows downhill past various stagnant bogs notable for their smells and muck. Other rivers run blood or salt tears. All are without nourishment for the barren land through which they pass. Their banks are either lined with stone or, like the channels of Malebolge, coated with "exhalations, [which] rising from below, / stuck to the banks, encrusting them with mold, / and so waged war against both eye and nose."[7] When Dante looks deeper he sees "people plunged in excrement that seemed / as if it had been poured from human privies."[8] Literal and figurative sewage is the burden of all infernal waters. The rivers Styx, Acheron, and Phlegethon drain toward the center of Hell, increasing their burden of tears, blood, sin, and excrement at each descending level. Later, on the Mountain of Purgatory, Dante also learns that the River Lethe, which originates in the Garden of Eden, collects the cleansed sins of Purgatory before it, too, makes its way to Hell. The sins and excretions of penitent and impenitent alike mingle in the frozen cesspool of Cocytus where Dante's great sewage-laden rivers converge. In Hell, the polluted rivers become instruments of torture for those who have polluted them.

Hell's most distinctive characteristic is its hostility to life. Dante's last view of earthly wildlife is an encounter with a leopard, a lion, and a wolf shortly before entering Hell. Although they seem threatening, Dante reacts only in fear of their power and is not repelled by their appearance. The leopard is "very quick and lithe" and has a "spotted hide"; the lion is a dignified animal with its "head held high and ravenous with hunger"; and even the she-wolf is not hideous, but merely seems "to carry every craving in her leanness."[9] The lean agility of these predators is in sharp contrast to the obese and malformed animals that occupy Hell. The few animals in Hell are grotesque mythical beasts with humanoid features such as Cerberus, the three-headed doglike creature whose "eyes are blood-red; greasy, black, his beard; / his belly bulges, and his hands are claws;"[10] the Harpie birds whose "wings are wide, their necks and faces human; / their feet taloned, their great bellies feathered;"[11] or the Monster Geryon whose face was "that of a just man" but whose body is a serpent's trunk with a scorpion's stinger at its tail.[12] Hell's fauna are grotesque fusions of animal and human forms; genuine animals are not to be found there.

The flora of Hell is similarly maimed, its plants stunted, deformed, leafless, and lifeless. The third circle is "an open plain / that banishes all green things from its bed," and is surrounded by "a wood of sorrow."[13] Such scenes are frequent in Hell, reminding the reader of the absence of light and water required by plant life. Hell's most memorable plants are perhaps the trees that encase the suicides on the seventh circle: "No green leaves in that forest, only black; / no branches straight and smooth, but knotted, gnarled; / no fruits were there, but briers bearing poison."[14] Like the animals of Hell, these plants are images of distorted humanity. When Dante plucks a twig, words and blood bubble forth together to reveal the vegetative soul of Pier della Vigna, a statesman who had taken his own life when his political fortunes fell. Suicide means refusing to face the changes and difficulties that go with being human. This tree is a man who has sought and attained a stunted vegetative existence. Aside from such images, Hell is without greenery or flowers.

All landscapes in Hell are bleak, and all natural processes are diseased. Natural elements normally associated with beauty have become ugly reminders of human destructiveness. Although Hell is an alpine setting that taxes the climbing skills of Dante the Pilgrim, scaling its crags provides no more satisfaction than climbers would find from exploring an open-pit mine. Such anachronistic comparisons are hard to avoid when reading the *Inferno*. Modern oil slicks are suggested by Dante's description of the boiling pitch in which the barrators suffer, especially when Dante compares the souls to wild ducks, falcons, and hawks and shows them trapped in petroleum: "there was no way they could get out; / their wings were stuck, enmeshed in glue-like pitch."[15] We need not speculate on Dante's mystic premonition of twentieth-century problems; it is enough to recognize that his fourteenth-century attempt to imagine the worst possible human environment describes many of the environmental horrors that have only recently been experienced.

Hell is also overpopulated. Overcrowding is the first misery Dante encounters on his guided tour. Just inside the gate he sees the mob of neutrals: "So long a file / of people—I should never have believed / that death could have unmade so many souls."[16] As his journey continues, Dante discovers that everyone in Hell is crowded, spaceless, jammed together with others from whom there is no escape. Trapped togetherness is one of Hell's most characteristic images, repeated on many levels among souls whose torment is to share a small space with one another: Farinata and Cavalcante in their tiny tomb, Ulysses and Diomede as forked tongues of a single flame, Ugolino and Ruggieri gnawing one another while frozen fast in the ice. High population density is one of Hell's most painful miseries.

As citizens are said always to get the kind of government they deserve, Dante provides his characters with the kind of environment they have earned by their actions. The inhabitants of Hell are people who would make the headlines in any century: political and religious leaders, businessmen and scientists, sex queens, heroes and cowards, and freaks. They have in common a single-minded egotism that sets them apart from others and makes their actions seem abnormally significant or dramatic. They are people who have focused their attention upon some fragment of the world, whether in an admirable or reprehensible way, and made it their own.

Readers are often troubled to find some of their favorite mythical or historical figures in Dante's Hell. Achilles, Dido, Cleopatra, and several famous popes are there, together with others whose names are not well known but whose characters are easily admired: Farinata, the competent and powerful politician who puts the welfare of his party above all else; Francesca, the beautiful woman whose passionate love has made her the victim of murder by a jealous husband; Cavalcante, the dedicated parent who sacrifices himself for his son; Pier della Vigna, the faithful and dedicated civil servant who lost his identity when a bureaucratic shake-up cost him his job. The reader's easy sympathy for such people expresses the recognition that most of us are equally susceptible to such misfortunes, but it also obscures for many reasons the essential fact that all of these souls have limited their vision of the world to the confines of their personal interests and activities. They all assume that their private experience of the world is somehow definitive of its basic nature. That is why the sign at the gate says "Abandon every hope, who enter here." The souls in Hell are those who have lost the capacity for seeing themselves in the context of a larger perspective. They will never discover the true reasons for their suffering.

The people in Dante's Hell do not really know they are there. Like many moderns, their creation of a joyless environment results from the actions in which they take greatest pride, and they fail to see any causal relationship between those actions and their consequences. The souls do not know they are in Hell any more than Dante's contemporaries knew that the Earth revolves around the sun, for recognition of either fact would necessarily lead to the correction of error. They are prevented from knowing their true state by the pride they take in their uniqueness and specialized talent. Francesca loves being in love, Farinata is proud of his political party, Ugolino lives only to punish his enemy. They feel the pain of their existence, but are at a loss to explain its source. Some, like Francesca and Pier, think they are punished unjustly by a tyrannical God and so solicit pity; others, like Farinata and Satan himself, are proud figures who nobly bear their pain and show only contempt for their surroundings. Scorning the condition of one's soul is one of the meanings of Hell. Many are like addicts in denial, unable to take responsibility for their own addiction, and facile at explaining their unhappiness by pointing to everything except its cause. Hell is a colossal image of spiritual irony, where the means for relief from pain are not discernible because the pain is so intense.

Souls in Dante's Hell are not punished by God because they have broken the rules of medieval Christian morality. No God and no rules appear in the *Comedy*. Technical sin is of small interest to Dante, who is concerned about the motivations of human actions and their appropriateness to the context in which they occur. Suicide damns Pier because it is an abdication of responsibility, but Cato, also a suicide, has a place of honor in Purgatory because he sacrificed his life in the service of human freedom. Sexuality becomes a prison for Francesca but is the power that Beatrice uses to lure Dante toward Paradise. No action or event in Dante's poem has any meaning apart from its context, and it is the context itself, not any external authority, that governs its consequences. The people in Hell are there because they have "lost the good of the intellect."[17] The mind permits humans to understand the world and to act for its welfare and their own. The refusal to understand is its own punishment.

It would have been easy for Dante to represent Hell as a fearful wilderness setting where nature is symbolic of evil and hostile to humans. Much precedent for such an image was ready at hand in medieval tales and legends and in church dogma. Dante's decision to describe Hell as an environment polluted by people and excluding all wild or natural forms is a deliberate innovation that he executes with care and consistency. It is necessary to his idea that humans are the responsible creators of the world in which they must live.

Purgatorio

The first line of the *Purgatorio* proclaims that Dante's journey now moves "across more kindly waters." He has also "left behind the air of death / that had afflicted both my sight and breast,"[18] and the sky is now clear from zenith to horizon. Purgatory is an environment congenial to life, where trees give shade, dew falls, and grass grows. Air, water, and vegetation are in a healthy state, not cultivated and managed by human gardeners, but self-maintained.

Purgatory is a real mountain. The souls Dante meets there are fellow climbers who share a common cause, ascent, and who collaborate to achieve it. They work hard together all day and gather in the evening for friendly conversation. Like good climbers everywhere, they know that the purpose of climbing is to master oneself, not to conquer the mountain. Purgatory is "the mountain whose ascent / delivers man from sin"[19] not because it has magical powers but because climbers increase their strength as they ascend by their own efforts.

Hell was shaped like a funnel where vision was directed increasingly inward with each stage of descent; on Purgatory, perspectives become broader with each higher level. Dante exploits the relationship between optical and figurative vision to show that Purgatory is a place of learning. The pilgrim's meetings with groups of souls become impromptu seminars on some aspect of nature or experience, moderated generally by professor Virgil, Dante's guide. The curriculum of Purgatory includes whatever can be understood by the intellect.

Virgil is a person "who ponders as he labors, / who's always ready for the step ahead."[20] He is a competent scholar and a well-informed scientist. In addition to his running commentary that explains the phenomena of Purgatory and includes excursions into such topics as anatomy and physiology,

Virgil frequently instructs his pupil in the techniques and limitations of intellectual investigation. His characteristic admonition to Dante, "Your mind must not attend to just one part,"[21] emphasizes the multiple aspects of knowledge and the subtle relationships among its many parts. His lectures are factual expositions of what is known about humanity and the world, not speculation into mysteries. His advice is "Confine yourselves, o humans, to the *quia*"[22]—to the *that* of facts and experiences—rather than search for the *why* of final causes.

Short of the mountaintop, Virgil pauses to conduct a graduation ceremony for his pupil. "I crown and miter you over yourself,"[23] he tells Dante as he bids him farewell. "I've brought you here through intellect and art; / from now on, let your pleasure be your guide."[24] There is a limit to the help that professors can give, and Virgil has reached it. Only when he is fully knowledgeable about the world does Dante become free to let his instincts guide him.

Dante often expresses a belief that instincts govern the behavior of living creatures, including people. The exposition of this idea occurs first in one of Virgil's lectures on love, and is later expanded by Beatrice in Paradise. Virgil first equates love with pleasure, explaining that "the soul, which is created quick to love, / responds to everything that pleases."[25] Dante is troubled to hear that love is a manifestation of innate desires, for that suggests to him that humans are not responsible for their actions and therefore that no free will exists. Virgil cannot solve this problem, but he explains it as best reason can manage:

> Every substantial form, at once distinct
> from matter and conjoined to it, ingathers
> the force that is distinctively its own,
>
> a force unknown to us until it acts—
> it's never shown except in its effects,
> just as green boughs display the life in plants.
>
> And thus man does not know the source of his
> intelligence of primal notions and
> his tending toward desire's primal objects:
>
> both are in you just as in bees there is
> the honey-making urge; such primal will
> deserves no praise, and it deserves no blame.[26]

As plants produce leaves and as bees make honey, so humans behave according to innate desires, the origins of which are unknown. "Innate" (*innata*) is Dante's word, not an imposition of modern terminology upon Dante's text. Virgil has more to say about the role of intellect, which has an influence upon innate desires, but leaves the fuller exposition of that matter to Beatrice, as we will. Virgil merely distinguishes between two types of love, "natural or mental" and specifies that "the natural is always without error, / but mental love may choose an evil object / or err through too much or too little vigor."[27] The sins suffered from in Hell and Purgatory are all results of excessive, defective, or misdirected love; that is, of the harmful use of the mind to distort natural behavior. Virgil sounds like a modern cognitive ethologist in this and in his assertion that the actions of organisms arise from within the organisms themselves and are not the products either of divine will or of environmental determinism.

Souls rise in Purgatory when they succeed in reconciling their minds with their instincts, or in Dante's terms, their will with their desire. No jailers watch over them and no rules of penance are imposed to determine their qualifications for ascent. Statius, a soul just freed from the circle of prodigality, explains to Dante that "the will alone is proof of purity / and, fully free, surprises soul into / a change of dwelling place"[28] as soon as its innate desires are consonant with its conscious will concerning the particular sin with which it has been afflicted. All human suffering in Hell and Purgatory is the consequence of misusing the powers of the mind to limit or distort natural processes that are "always without error." The main difference is that souls in Purgatory have accurately recognized the source of their suffering, and so can seek to correct it, while souls in Hell remain blind to the causes of their pain.

The final environment of Purgatory is the Earthly Paradise on the mountaintop. Dante finds there no pastoral pleasure garden or manicured rural landscape, but a "forest—alive with green, divine."[29] It is like a dense tropical forest where the sun never reaches the ground. Something prompted Dante to avoid the standard Christian image of a cultivated and sunny Eden where nature is subordinate to humanity and to describe instead a complex landscape which, "depending on / the nature of its land and sky, conceives and bears from diverse powers, diverse trees."[30] Diversity is the clearest feature of Dante's Eden, felt in everything from the ground "full of every seed"[31] to the intricate pageantry that displays the entire medieval bestiary of symbolic griffons, foxes, eagles, and dragons, along with the complicated forms of church and state on Earth and the spiritual transcendence represented by Christ and the heavenly eyes of Beatrice. This Eden is no place of quiet repose, but a busy meeting ground where the processes of nature coalesce with those of society, the human intellect, and the powers of spirit in active interchange. It is here that Beatrice, called by Virgil "the light between your mind and truth,"[32] takes over the guidance of Dante through the even more complex experiences ahead of him.

Paradiso

Dante's Paradise is not properly an environment at all, but a state of being experienced by those who know themselves to be in harmony with the principles and processes of creation. For this reason it is the most difficult part of the poem for many modern readers to understand. Paradise represents principles and ideas freed from their dependence upon particular entities: love that transcends attachment to things, process without active agents, relationships without objects, plurality without singularity, truth without facts, comedy without tragedy, play without games, and pure light perceived directly rather than reflected from surfaces. "On the sun I set / my sight more than we usually do," Dante announces at the beginning;[33] Paradise is where he learns to look directly at the sources of life, not by wearing protective glasses or studying reflected images, but by perfecting his vision.

Virgil conducted Dante as far as good scientific analysis can conduct human beings, to the point of factual understanding of the structure and meaning of the world. The vision of integration that Dante finds in Paradise is suprascientific, although inclusive of the science of Dante's time and consistent with it. It is also suprahuman in the sense that it passes beyond the levels of human experience that language is suited to describe. Dante reminds his readers that "Passing beyond humanity [*transhumanar*] cannot be / worded,"[34] because words, however figurative or abstract, depend upon their relationships to things and events. Virgil, the inquiring and comprehending mind, is no longer enough to serve Dante's needs, and he is superseded by an image that combines rational knowledge with spiritual insight and wordless wonder, the beautiful woman Beatrice.

The role played by the historical Beatrice in Dante's life and her symbolic role in the *Comedy* are subtle and complex. In the *Paradiso*, Dante uses her to represent a fulfilled human being who has realized intellectually and spiritually her true relationship to reality and who thus radiates beauty united with intelligence. She has everything that Virgil had, plus the powers of emotional and aesthetic attraction that make her loved as well as respected.

Like a good scientist, Beatrice believes that "All things, among themselves, / possess an order."[35] Her concept of order, however, is a rich synthesis of material and spiritual reality that has nothing mechanistic about it. Beatrice is a vitalist who believes that there is an instinct (*instinto*) in all things: "This is the motive force in mortal creatures; / this binds the earth together, makes it one."[36] Her doctrine is derived from scholastic theology, which defines God's love as a kind of divine mucilage holding the world together and governing all change and growth. Unlike some church dogmatists, Beatrice emphasizes that the instinct for order is *internal* to the creatures of the universe, not regulated by a divine intelligence, and that it operates the same in all forms of life: "Not only does the shaft shot from this bow / strike creatures lacking intellect, but those / who have intelligence, and who can love."[37] The metaphor that likens instinct to a bow and creatures to arrows reaffirms the belief expressed throughout the *Comedy* that the power of life is internal to living creatures, and that humans alone have the ability to misdirect that power through errors of the intellect. As the souls in Hell aimed toward selfish aggrandizement and those in Purgatory learned of higher targets, so the souls in Paradise have achieved the unity of the bow of instinct (desire) and the arrow of intellect (will) centered on the target of universal order.

Throughout the *Paradiso*, great emphasis is placed upon diversity as a necessary condition for stability and order. When Beatrice instructs Dante in the complex organization of Paradise, she reminds him that "diverse virtue makes diverse alloy"[38] and that he should not expect to find here the relative simplicity of Hell and Purgatory. The soul of Charles Martel later extends this principle to include behavioral as well as structural diversity, arguing that humans must "live in diverse ways for diverse tasks" as other natural creatures do.[39] He concludes his explanation of diversity with an admonition: "If the world below would set its mind / on the foundation Nature lays as base / to follow, it would have its people worthy."[40] Although this argument is often interpreted as an instance of the medieval effort to hold people in the social status of their birth, it is evident from the context that Dante intends also to establish diversity of human and natural elements as a necessary condition for stability.

Dante's *Paradiso* is not an abstract conception that rejects the validity of physical or sensual experience. Much medieval literature shuns the senses and the world, but not Dante. His Paradise is a place where bodily experience is perfected, not rejected. However spiritual or symbolic Beatrice may be, Dante never lets the reader forget that she is also a beautiful woman whose appearance thrills him as often as do her words. And when Beatrice explains the resurrection of the body, she is happy to assure Dante that on Judgment Day, "the body's organs will have force / enough for all in which we can delight."[41] Paradise is no ascetic retreat, but a completed experience in which sensuality is appreciated for its full meaning and context and therefore enjoyed more fully than when it is pursued only for personal gratification.

Dante never rejects the world even when he perceives its smallness from the threshold of the Empyrean. His astronaut's view of Earth, like those we have acquired technologically in our time, reminds him that the Earth is a small element of a larger system, a dependent part rather than an end in itself. "I saw this globe in such a way that I / smiled at its meager image," says Dante.[42] There is no scorn in this view, but rather compassion for the Earth's inhabitants on their "little threshing floor."[43] Dante's entry into Paradise is not an escape from the Earth, but the acquisition of a larger perspective from which to understand it.

Even Dante's final beatific vision is an integration of the world's parts, one of which is humanity. There is no ordering deity in human form controlling the universe from the upper reaches of Paradise, but only pure light, dazzling in its clarity and intensity. Dante's visual schooling as he has passed through the realms of being has prepared him to gaze at the source of light directly, and even to make out some images within it:

> O grace abounding, through which I presumed
> to set my eyes on the Eternal Light
> so long that I spent all my sight on it!
> In its profundity I saw—ingathered
> and bound by love into one single volume—
> what, in the universe, seems separate, scattered:

substances, accidents, and dispositions
as if conjoined—in such a way that what
I tell is only rudimentary.
　　I think I saw the universal shape
which that knot takes; for, speaking this, I feel
a joy that is more ample.[44]

The universal form is a complex of relationships, inclusive of all life, thought, and spirit. As Dante stares, his vision improves further and he begins to see circles and colors and movements that appear to be "painted with our effigy."[45] The image of humanity, in some obscure way, is a part of the image of universal form, and Dante strains in an effort to see "the way in which our human effigy / suited the circle and found place in it— / and my own wings were far too weak for that."[46] Humanity is somehow amidst the substances, accidents, and relationships of universal order, but Dante's vision and his poem end with the unanswerable question of how, precisely, humanity fits in.

Dante's Paradise, and especially the beatific vision at its height, resembles an ultimate climax ecosystem. Ecologists sometimes object to the use of the term *climax* because it suggests finality and completeness, states that are foreign to natural processes, and because it tends to encourage people to think of nature in static terms. But the climax of a literary work is the moment when all themes, moods, and ideas unite in a flash of insight and their genuine relationships suddenly become clear. It is not a sustainable insight, but is followed inevitably by a denouement, returning the reader once more to the more prosaic world of fragmentary events and their uncertain consequences. Literary, metaphysical, sexual, and ecological climaxes are not permanently frozen states of being, but momentary epiphanies from which less intense and less perfect events must follow. Dante must return from his high vision to a desk somewhere in tortured Italy so that he can write a poem telling of what he has seen.

Play in Paradise

Play is a dependable indicator of mental and spiritual good health. The souls in Dante's Hell are mildly neurotic to pathological people, all of them with enemies, compulsive goals, and agendas to fulfill. Souls in Purgatory work hard, too, trying to overcome their shortcomings and build their strengths. The souls in Dante's Paradise are also very busy, but their time is full of joy. They are without goals and objectives, and they are free of ambitions. Being in Paradise means feeling fully engaged, genuinely pleased with oneself, strong in relationships, with spirit, mind, and body bent on fulfilling themselves and those they love. Paradise is for the playful.

Modern experience confirms Dante's comic classification. Those with the least play in their lives are people like convicted felons, murderers, drunk drivers, and others who probably had little or poor play in childhood, and have long since lost the capacity to play for the sake of play. Somewhat above them, in the equivalent of Dante's Purgatory, are the hard-working people whose lives are devoted to tangible objectives like wealth, property, power, or status. Their lives may be honorable, but they are subject to great stress and endless pendulum swings of highs and lows.

The happiest people, those Dante would find in Paradise, are also some of the most successful and healthy people in our world. They are the Nobel Prize winners, the great artists and scientists, the leaders who act out of hope and vision. They are all those people who are continually astonished that they are paid for what they do, because they so love doing it. They are the happy people whose work is play.

To understand what it means to be in Paradise, we can begin by reflecting upon those times when life has seemed at its best. The souls in Dante's Paradise show states of being and feeling that many people have experienced at one time or another:

* They feel perfect clarity of mind, with no impediments between subject and object, and are confident in the accuracy of their perceptions.
* They feel perfectly understood and accepted by those around them.
* They feel genuine empathy for the joys and pains of others.
* They feel perfectly free to do and be what they choose.
* They feel that they are doing work of excellent quality that is almost effortless for them.
* They know that the work they are doing is exactly the right work for them.
* They feel unimpededly joyful.
* They experience a powerful sense of interconnectedness with others and with the world.

* They are aware that they are in the presence of great beauty.
* They experience complete sensual fulfillment.
* They feel fully loved and fully loving.
* They feel that they genuinely understand the meaning of their lives.
* They know that the things they most desire are really the things that they ought to have.
* Their best fantasies agree with their best judgment.

All of us know that experiences like these are possible, because we have felt them for ourselves during our great moments. Dante's *Paradiso* is simply a place where these are normal for everyone, all the time. This is the highest state of play.

Dante's Comic Way

The twentieth-century French philosopher Jacques Maritain spoke of Dante's "innocence" and of his "luck."[47] Dante was innocent in the sense that he unashamedly assumed that his private experience was symbolic of the life of all humanity. His love of Beatrice stood for all love, his life in politics illustrated the meaning of politics, and his vision of universal order revealed genuine cosmic integration. Dante's poem is unique in its fusion of the intensely personal with the highest levels of abstraction, and in its convincing demonstration that the two are compatible.

Dante was "lucky" because his life coincided with a climactic moment in medieval Christianity just prior to its disintegration. Dante's time made available what Maritain calls "existential certainties" that affirmed that the intricate complexities of the world are intelligible, and that all life is integrated according to principles that we must recognize and adapt to if we hope to attain fulfillment. Dante's world permitted these basic assumptions more fully than any period since, and permitted Dante to construct in his poem the last image of an integrated universe before the fragmentations of the modern world emerged.

From a modern, scientific perspective, Dante's medieval world appears to be drastically misinformed about the nature of things. Dante lived in a world that did not know about nuclear power, about the profound changes that technology was to make upon human perceptions, about indeterminacy in physics and neurosis in the subconscious, about space travel and the evolution of humans from animal origins. Nevertheless, modern readers discover that Dante describes accurately the specific characteristics of their own felt experience. The nature of human pain and joy has not changed in the seven centuries since Dante, but the world has come to resemble Hell more than ever.

Medieval Christianity provided people with a way to think about the world and to respond to its conditions as participants in an order larger than themselves. However complex, the world appeared to have a meaningful structure, and a human being's welfare appeared to depend upon understanding that structure and coordinating one's own life with it. During the succeeding centuries, Western civilization has operated largely on the assumption that the world must be shaped and managed to conform to human needs and interests. The consequences of that assumption are evident in the disruption of the natural environment and in the disorder of the modern soul.

Dante explained the title of his poem by referring to the classic definition of comic form as the passage from pain to pleasure: "At the beginning it is horrible and fetid, for it is Hell; and in the end it is prosperous, desirable, and gracious, for it is Paradise." It is also comic in that its language is "lax and humble," as opposed to the elevated and dignified discourse of tragic poetry.[48] But the poem is also comic in the sense used throughout this book: it is an image of human adaptation to the world and acceptance of its given conditions without escape, rebellion, or egotistic insistence upon human centrality.

Thomas Mann's Felix Krull and Dante's pilgrim have in common their belief that life is an art form. Dante's love of all life causes him to see the cosmos as an all-encompassing work of art in which all creatures can find fulfillment. This is not the tragic-pastoral vision of a world of raw materials destined to receive artistic form through skillful human manipulation, but the comic-picaresque image of a beautiful world that human creativeness should complement. Felix Krull's motto, "He who truly loves the world must shape himself to please it," describes accurately the meaning of Dante's philosophy and the strategy of his art.

8 * Toying with a Play Ethic

We mammals, along with the birds, have been playing and living comic lives for some two hundred million years. There is no need to learn how to play, for that knowledge is deeply embedded in our bones and genes. Play is as natural as breathing, and the comic urge for normalcy is as basic as the need for balance. If we nevertheless fail to play and feel off-balance much of the time, it must be because we have bent ourselves terribly out of shape, imposing crushing mental and cultural burdens that make gravity seem more important than levity.

I often suggest that people write a play history of their lives, including the places and playmates of their own childhood and as much information as possible about play in the lives of their parents and grandparents. That exercise led me to contemplate my two grandfathers, and to appraise their very different play legacies for my life. Writing one's play history makes it possible to revisit childhood play, and sometimes to regain it. It also provides an occasion to reflect upon the disappearance of play from our lives. What were the events and influences that impeded or forbade play as we grew older? The loss of play is a grievous price to pay, especially since we probably received nothing nearly so valuable in exchange.

This book has been partly an attempt to write a play history for humanity, or at least for Western culture. Our ancestors who invented tragedy some three thousand years ago made a direct assault upon the comic way. What we gained from that was a new sense of human dignity, and a belief that suffering could ennoble us. The tragic view also persuaded us that we could rise above nature and control our own destiny by the power of character and individual will. Those powerful messages from the tragic tradition have persuaded us that we need not live by the restraints that govern other forms of life. Thus we have become powerful, self-absorbed, and estranged from the Earth.

Another direct attack upon the comic way grew from the Protestant revolution that began some four hundred years ago to develop the ideology of the work ethic. Divine favor was believed to shine upon those whose lives were consumed by work, and wealth and power came to those who banished play from their lives. Beyond its religious impact, the work ethic has obviously been important to business, industry, politics, and much of public life, especially in America, where the Puritan version of the work ethic was present at the founding of most institutions and traditions. My grandfather Sinus Block brought both Protestant fundamentalism and the tragic tradition with him from Germany, and he arrived to find reinforcement from American Puritanism for his values and lifestyle.

Yet my other grandfather, Joe Meeker, lived in about the same place at the same time, seemingly immune to both tragedy and the work ethic. He was also, of course, immune to power and wealth. There have always been people who live apart from the power structures of society, following the comic way toward a playground of their own. There is a comic underground, perhaps, where the ancient ways of life that we share with other species can be realized.

The children of my grandparents were my parents. My mother, Annamae, like her father before her, played to win. She craved respect and power, and was always a dangerous person to be around when either was threatened. Winning, for her, meant weakening her enemy and affirming her strength. She usually had a clear goal of some kind in her sights, such as a new home or a big income or the defeat of someone she feared or hated. Her friendships were generally with people who could do some good for her. Her enemies were spoken of as the worst sort of evil people, hateful to God and Mom alike. Mostly, her world was polarized into good and evil camps. She was righteous in her moral indignation over those who failed to measure up to her standards: that included people who competed with her in any way, those she considered lazy or dirty, most black people, her younger sister, the mates chosen by her children, and all men. She was a profoundly unhappy woman, and was bitter up to her death at age eighty-six.

Russell, my father, seems rather to have seen things as a muddle that had to be dealt with a piece at a time. Working, whether on the farm or for the government, was never an end in itself or the means to an end, but merely a strategy for getting along in life. He had no particular ambitions or goals that I knew of, but took his pleasure from participating in activities that were their own reward: music, gardening, conversation. He loved to argue, especially with his brothers, but the arguments never determined a winner or loser, and usually ended in the sharing of a drink. I remember a conversation he had with an insurance salesman who visited our home. The salesman argued that the policy he was selling would give Russell's family security after his death; he said that Russell might walk out the door tomorrow morning and get run over by a truck, leaving his family with a lot of money. "Oh," said Dad, "I could never be that lucky." He simply didn't take wealth or ambition seriously. That was enough to put him on Annamae's list of evil people.

Their unlikely marriage lasted fifteen years before it ended mercifully in divorce. Annamae never remarried, and always had plenty to say about the wickedness of all men. Russell had a happy second marriage, and also lived to be eighty-six. After his funeral, the mourners gathered for a meal together. Then Dad's only surviving siblings, also in their eighties, recalled the days of the Meeker Orchestra, when all the family played together daily. Howard, although he suffered from Alzheimer's and could scarcely manage a conversation, had remembered to bring along a harmonica. Mabel, also weak and ill, made her way to the piano and the two started playing dance tunes. Within minutes we were all dancing and singing together. The spirit of play survived that funeral, helping us all to return to normal.

Avoiding Purposes

A modern twist on the work ethic has been added by something called MBO, or Management By Objectives, a technique that requires every project to be directed toward clearly stated goals and objectives. Every action is supposed to be purposeful toward attaining those goals, with no time or energy wasted on peripheral activities. MBO has been influential in education, business, and government because it promises efficiency of production and clarity of purpose. It rigidly screens out spontaneity, imagination, and surprise as parts of the creative process, and it is the enemy of anything so useless as play.

I have always been pleased that the framers of the American Constitution did not know about MBO as they wrote their great document. The Constitution provides only a statement of the beliefs and values that we hold as a people, and it describes the processes by which we will make decisions. It did not set goals such as the extermination of Indian peoples, or the bridging of the continent in eighty years, or the Gross Domestic Product at the end of the next century. I take comfort from noting that evolution also does not operate according to goals and objectives. Both ecological succession and natural selection are aimless processes that work with whatever conditions and forms are present in opportunistic and inventive ways to create new forms that will be appropriate to the conditions of life in a given time and place. They are like play in their purposelessness and spontaneity. The comic way may be inefficient and wasteful, as evolution and succession are, but these processes have created the beauty of biological diversity, including humans and their playful minds.

Is it possible that someone who has been schooled in the work ethic can learn to play in the comic way? Can Sinus Block learn to dance to the music of Grandpa Joe? My experience tells me that this is possible, for I have seen it happen many times. I have watched on several occasions as Fred Donaldson, play master, has gently talked groups of more than a hundred people, ages sixteen through eighty, through a series of movements that eventually find them all on the floor, rolling over and playing with one another much as puppies and kittens do. There are a few who withdraw early from these exercises in fear, and never allow themselves the freedom to play, but even these are often able to participate on a second attempt after they have seen that no one was injured or abused. I have also seen videotapes of Fred doing this exercise in South Africa with a mixed group of black and white people, none of whom have ever touched a person of the other skin color before. Watching these people play freely and joyfully together makes it dramatically clear that this play is anything but trivial behavior.

A favorite activity of mine is the Playpole, which is nothing more than a Maypole done in some other month than May. This ancient ritual dates to preagricultural times and is rooted in the need to celebrate the importance of trees and forests for all life. A pole, representing the forest, is erected and adorned with multicolored ribbons. The people then make two concentric circles around the pole, with each person holding a ribbon, and the circles move in opposite directions, each person alternately passing the ribbon over and under the person facing them as they move. Once set in motion, preferably to lively music, there is nothing participants can do but play with one another, and no way to avoid laughter and joyful dancing. The most staid and compulsive people emerge from a Playpole experience feeling joyful as children at play, and proud of the beautiful woven design that their play has created upon the pole. I have left Playpoles in Alaskan glaciers, Southwest deserts, and many other places as testimony to moments of play. For years after, they bring smiles to people who discover them.

Playtalk

The songs of birds have fascinated the human imagination forever, I suppose. Elaborate and insightful scientific studies interpret and analyze birdsong, but I find myself more interested in its mythology, and in the mirror that the birds provide to help us to understand human relationships. I think birdsong, like good human conversation, is a healthy kind of play.

The mythic meaning of birdsong, I think, is a musical affirmation of place and relationship. I like to imagine that the basic message the birds keep sending back and forth is something like, "I'm here; where are you?" It is a message of substance. "I'm here" is a statement of identity: this is me, an autonomous self who has a place in the world. It may also convey something about the state of the caller: I'm feeling sexy, or lonely, or angry, or frightened. The second part of the call, "where are you?" is about the relationship between your place and mine: are you near or far? Can we get together? Will you please get out of my territory? It may also say something about the state of our relationship: I wish you were here, or I'm here for you if you need me, or don't you dare cross that line. "I'm here; where are you?" is the essential stuff of all conversation and of all mythology, as we continually try to give expression to our sense of who we are, where we are, and how we are related to our places and to the others around us. In those ways, human conversation is not much different from birdsong.

Conversation is more than just a swapping of verbal news; it is a biological exchange, not at all limited to language. We converse using all of our senses and every means of perception. So do all other living creatures, including the living Earth. We can dance our conversations, sing them, tootle them on a flute, waft perfumes and scents to one another, share the tastes of foods and spices, run our hands through one another's fur or feathers. To climb a mountain is to enter into reciprocal conversation with it. The universal topics of conversation are familiar to all creatures: How are you feeling? How are your relatives? What is your history? How do you earn your living? Where is your home? What are your hopes and fears? How is your love life? How is your health? Is there some way I can help you? If we take the trouble to ask these questions in the right way and are willing to listen attentively, every creature on Earth can join with us in conversation, however varied our languages may be.

Good conversation is neither serious nor trivial, but playful. It is not serious, as debate is, for it does not have rigid rules and does not aim at defeating an opponent. It is not trivial, as gossip is, for it concerns only the people who are conversing, not absent others. The best conversations are exchanges between free and equal persons, each speaking originally and spontaneously, exploring one another with no clear expectation of what may be discovered. With luck, their discoveries will be surprises leading to yet new discoveries. Such conversations play with language and meaning, and the participants play with and enjoy one another.

Languages of science and public affairs change rapidly to adapt to current trends and circumstances, but conversation seems to plod along in about the same way from century to century, oblivious to fashion. It is a level of discourse little affected by social and ideological change, perhaps because it depends less upon its content and meaning than do other forms of discourse. Two shoppers chatting in the supermarket checkout line are probably observing the same rules of conversation that were recognized by two Paleolithic hunters as they butchered a hunted animal in their equivalent of the supermarket. Conversations of those sorts are intimate exchanges among two or more persons, the main result of which is to reveal or renew the relationships among them.

Genuine conversation is not teaching or exhorting or preaching or counselling or therapy or argument, although aspects of all of these may be included incidentally at some point in the process of conversation. Content and meaning, in some strange way, are perhaps the least significant aspects of conversation, lagging far behind the importance of the form and process of the conversation and its influence upon the relationships among its participants.

Good conversation is characterized by feelings of equality among those who share in it, permitting each to speak with some confidence and power. It is a process where all are givers and all receivers, and no tally is kept of who is ahead. You can win or lose an argument, but there is no winning or losing in good conversation, where each appropriate move that is made is simply rewarded by the prize of continuing the conversation. It is an exchange of energies more than of information, a dance more than a march toward some destination. Words somehow become vehicles for more than just their meanings, conveying subtle invitations, appreciations, aversions, and alliances, and creating rhythms to be shared.

Conversation is very much a bodily affair. Its words seem less important for their semantic meanings than for the sensations they convey. Conversation often sounds like poetry, or looks like dance. Hands, eyes, lips, bodily movements, shoulder shrugs, shifting weight, raised eyebrows, wrinkled noses are a few of the bodily clues used to interpret the nuances of conversation. Once engaged in conversation, we look for consistency among the various means our partners use to convey themselves to us. A twitching eyelid or a shifting gaze can raise doubts about the genuineness of what is being said. Tiny signals that seem out of place or inconsistent are enough to jeopardize the flow of interaction and to raise barriers. Equally delicate leads can guide us toward joy and understanding.

At its best, conversation crosses the boundaries between us and permits us to feel that we are both parts of the same good and interesting process. This does not happen because of agreement, for we may disagree seriously and still value our conversation. It does not necessarily mean that we "understand" one another, for we may be mutually obscure and yet be thoroughly together in conversation. It need not even mean that we like one another, as long as some small measure of confidence and respect is present. When conversation works, it does mean that, at least for the moment, we are walking the same road together and helping one another along the way. What we share is a mutually-agreed-upon process and form for our relationship at this moment. If we are able to repeat a similar process at many different times, then we know we have found a friend, a spirit to depend upon. Friends help us to remember that the boundaries we live with most of the time are not absolute barriers.

Conversation is necessary for love to grow between two people, and without it, healthy love is difficult to sustain. The character of conversation between a man and a woman is an excellent indicator of how a sexual relationship between them might develop. Both conversation and sexuality require giving, receiving, sharing, touch and response, allowing and encouraging freedom of expression, enjoyment of surprise, mutual exploration, and the whole repertoire of relationships. Conversation sometimes seems almost like an essential kind of foreplay, without which no other kind should proceed.

Talking with the Rocks

Relationships between ourselves and the natural contexts of life are also revealed through subtle kinds of conversations. Talking with plants and animals feels like a genuine exchange, more often than not a reciprocal one. Cross-species communication may be rooted deeply in our hunting/gathering past, and it may not be limited to living creatures.

Not long ago I found myself helping to care for two young children, Bodie, a boy of eight, and his sister Bayley, a six-year-old. We lived together for about four years, and became good friends. One day Bodie came home from school feeling grumpy. He said very little, but went to his toolbox and got a hammer, then went outside. A few minutes later I heard sharp bangs coming from the base of the driveway about a hundred yards from the house. Beside the driveway is a large rock, about three feet in diameter, a glacial erratic left there by the most recent glaciation some ten thousand years ago. Bodie was beating the rock with his hammer as hard as he could, knocking off chips and defacing it.

I asked Bodie to stop hitting the rock, and explained to him that this rock was a particular friend of.mine. I told him what I knew about its geologic history, and gave him an account of some of my experiences with this rock (I had tried and failed to move it once). I also said that I thought he owed the rock an apology for the way he had treated it. Bodie looked at me is if I were a little crazy, then went on about his business.

About two days later, Bodie came home from school in a pensive mood, ate his snack, then put on his raincoat and went out into the drizzly day. Half an hour later, I noticed him sitting on the rock that he had abused. I got close enough to hear that he was talking to the rock, telling about the events of his day and how he was feeling. He stayed there perhaps ten minutes like that, then went to play at a neighbor's. I saw him visit the rock in this way several times over the next few weeks.

I'm not sure what went on in Bodie's mind. His relationship with the rock seemed to me private, and I didn't feel right about inquiring into it. Bodie does know what it feels like to be abused, to feel helpless while someone more powerful is venting anger upon you. He may, for a moment, have been able to see things from the rock's point of view. And he made his peace with the rock in the ancient way, by entering into conversation with it. I believe it was a two-way conversation, where Bodie received as much as he gave.

What all kinds of conversation seem to have in common is respectful boundary crossing. Whether the exchange is from one sleeping bag to another on a luminous night, from one bird's branch to another on a sunny morning, or from boy to rock on a rainy afternoon, the message seems always to be the nearly meaningless but absolutely crucial and playful conversation that begins with "I'm here; where are you?"

There is no reason we cannot answer that call and enter into conversation with the birds, and with many wild animals. Theodore Xenophon Barber concludes *The Human Nature of Birds* with an appendix on "Befriending Wild Birds," with advice on techniques of creating trust and friendship with birds, learning to play with them, and coming to know them as individual personalities with character traits, quirks, and varying levels of wisdom and intelligence, just like the people we know. The book also provides scores of examples of people all over the world who have successfully established friendships with birds. Barber attaches very great importance to making friends with the birds; he believes that human perception will change as we bond with other species, and that great transformations will follow: "By working with devotion and commitment to befriend birds and to understand their intelligence and personalities, you will be acting as part of a revolutionary movement that will change the consciousness and destiny of the human race."[1] It couldn't hurt the destiny of the birds, either.

Flocking and Playing

Flocks of birds may help us to understand how complex and beautiful systems are formed and maintained. Computer models created to mimic the behavior of flocking animals (birds, fish, herd animals) demonstrate that these intricate forms rest upon simple rules of behavior. One such program called "Boids" has birdlike images moving on a screen that also contains walls and other obstacles. The flock of boids flows endlessly, maintaining its integrity and avoiding obstacles just as a flock of real birds would do. The keys to this process are three simple behavioral commands, as M. Mitchell Waldrop reports them, that each boid is required to observe:

1   It tries to maintain a minimum distance from other objects in the environment, including other boids.
2   It tries to match velocities with boids in its neighborhood.
3   It tries to move toward the perceived center of the mass of boids in its neighborhood.[2]

The flocking effect is created solely by the relationship of each bird to those others that are nearby. No overall plan is needed to create a flock, for the flock is a natural consequence of individual behavior carried out locally. The third command, to move toward the perceived center of the mass, makes good sense, since the edges of a flock are dangerous places where predators are most likely to strike. The effect of all birds trying for the center is that those on the edges are not there for very long.

Flocking birds offer an attractive model for how large groups can create beauty and safety for themselves without having a Grand Plan. Perhaps significant social change can occur as a consequence of individuals interacting with one another locally and on a small scale. If so, playing together as individuals is one kind of behavior that should produce positive results for the surrounding society. It couldn't do a worse job than the competitive model has provided.

Storyplay

I enjoy being in the neighborhood of natural disasters, and have had fairly good luck at it. My home was in Alaska at the time of the great 9.3

earthquake of 1964 in Anchorage (I lived four hundred miles away in Fairbanks). I visited Washington State immediately after the eruption of Mt. St. Helens in 1980. During the Loma Prieta earthquake of 1989, I was in San Francisco, and I was in Southern California for the Northridge earthquake of 1994. Great movements like these are reminders that the Earth is alive, and is rearranging itself again. Events like these provide people with wonderful occasions for telling stories to one another. "Where were you when the big one hit?"—and off they go.

When people tell their disaster stories over and over again, the stories tend to improve with each repetition. Rough edges get rounded off, the right metaphors emerge gradually, and the stories find their appropriate focus, with main themes and subordinate images. They become stories of heroism, or divine intervention, or cosmic good fortune, or retribution, or cooperation among family and friends, or danger and survival. It often becomes clear that the stories have more to tell about the character and values of the storyteller than they do about the events of the disaster. This is the process of mythology in the making; those stories that speak of widely shared values, or tell of experiences that we can believe in and empathize with, are likely to survive and become the property of many people. That is how a cultural tradition grows.

The majority of such stories are comic, for they explain how the storytellers survived the disaster and restored normalcy to their lives. Others are melodramatic, eliciting sympathy for the storyteller or otherwise exploiting sentiments or tears. These are the ones favored by television journalists who cover disasters and court cases; any victim who can produce a tear on-camera is sure to make the evening news. Only rarely do disasters produce genuine tragic stories with a decisive battle between polarized good and evil, for such events are most often products of the imagination and are not to be found in natural processes or most human experience. The natural human response to adversity is to tell a comic story, as humans have been doing for millions of years.

Storytelling is one of the healthiest activities of the comic way. As long as our species has possessed language, we have used it to tell our stories to one another. Stories help to bond families together and create bodies of shared experiences. It is through storytelling that wisdom and knowledge are passed from elder to younger generations. Stories have always helped people to understand the dynamics of their natural environments, and to find benefits and avoid dangers. Human relations with animals are moderated by stories, and through stories, animals become symbolic creatures bearing cosmic and metaphysical meanings. What we have learned about good and bad behavior, manners and morals, customs and habits, gets transmitted through the stories we tell. Stories help to heal our wounds as we tell how we were wounded, just as they heal those who only listen to us. Story is essential to the comic purpose of affirming and perpetuating the normal conditions of life.

The Vitamin Effect

Cognitive ethologists speak of "the vitamin effect" to help explain how some forms of instinctual behavior came to exist. The idea originated with E. O. Wilson, who explained the biological evolution of vitamins as organs develop and make use of special biochemical compounds, which then become essential if the organism is to thrive. He gives the example of vitamin D, whose role it is to control the absorption of calcium from the intestine. Deprived of vitamins like that, the organism can usually survive, but at a lower level of well-being. Wilson then proposes the analogy that some forms of behavior may evolve just as vitamins do: "Behavioral elements involved in socialization become increasingly dependent on experience for normal development."[3] Play, conversation, storytelling, and other parts of what I have been calling the comic way may contribute to the mental and spiritual health of organisms in much the way that vitamins enhance biological health.

In a pinch, we can get along without our comic vitamins, sometimes for extended periods of time. Their absence may cause nothing more serious than minor depression or occasional fits of anger and despair. We may even argue that they are frivolous, trivial, or wicked, as proponents of the work ethic have often said. Or, as the tragic tradition does, we may simply conceive of the world with a polarized perspective that ignores the comic way as irrelevant to great events and passions. Yet in our better moments, we know that life feels best when we have generous doses of conversation, storytelling, play, and comedy. These are parts of our evolutionary history that help us to be whole, multidimensional, fulfilled creatures.

Just as vitamins do not make a complete diet, so the comic way does not account for all of life's experiences. Much of our time is necessarily spent competing, earning a living, mating, rearing children, fighting, feeling misery and despair, and living the full range and repertoire of human behavior and experience. But in the midst of all that, a recommended daily amount of play, say an hour or two, can balance our mental diet.

Having Enough

Bears, they say, are more likely to play when the salmon are running. The preconditions that are necessary for play to occur are measures of health in just about every kind of system, human and natural. There must be enough energy in the form of food and strength so that some can be expended for purposes other than bare survival. There must be enough freedom so that individuals can choose how to behave, and feel free to use some mental power for imagination rather than always coping with threats and dangers. Healthy, strong individuals who have a small surplus and a relatively safe environment are those who can afford to satisfy their need to play. The same is true of groups and societies; those that provide for their members enough of life's basic needs and essential freedoms can expect to find play as a regular feature. For individuals, societies, and ecosystems, the presence of play is one of the clearest measures of health and well being.

All of the elements of the comic way tend to spread to others, insinuating joy where it was previously absent. Conversation has a way of leaping around among persons, as it does at parties and celebratory gatherings. Storytelling always begets storytelling. It is difficult to watch others at play without wanting to join them. This is not only a human phenomenon, for researchers have consistently noticed that animals at play often are imitated by other animals.[4] So wherever it is possible to initiate a playful activity, it will have a good chance of replicating itself through other parts of its system.

A Play Ethic

The one thing that the comic way does not need is a set of rules. Comedy and play are always defined by the particular contexts in which they occur, not by rules and laws. Olympic athletes who are locked in close competition in their sport may still be playing in their hearts. Musicians who have spent years in drudging practice become free to play when their skills are sufficiently internalized and automated. So any statement of a play ethic must necessarily be loose, negotiable, and subject to daily revision.

A play ethic is anything but trivial, although it may be somewhat child-like. It cannot guide us toward the acquisition of power over others or over events, and it is unlikely to create wealth or status, as the work ethic has done. Play rather grows from our sense of freedom. It produces strength and skill for the players, stimulates the imagination, and encourages agility and self-confidence.

As the Puritans articulated the work ethic, so now it is our privilege to give voice to a new ethic of play. If we were to have a Playbill of Rights, it might include the following:

* All players are equal, or can be made so.
* Boundaries are well observed by crossing them.
* Novelty is more fun than repetition.
* Rules are negotiable from moment to moment.
* Risk in pursuit of play is worth it.
* The best play is beautiful and elegant.
* The purpose for playing is to play, nothing else.

Notes

Chapter 2

1 James P. Carse, *Finite and Infinite Games: A Vision of Life as Play and Possibility* (New York: Ballantine Books, 1986).

2 Carse, 3.

3 Carse, 8.

4 Robert Fagen, *Animal Play Behavior* (New York: Oxford University Press, 1981).

5 Fagen, 218–219.

6 Robert Axelrod, *The Evolution of Cooperation* (New York: Basic Books, 1984).

7 Axelrod, 173.

8 Axelrod, 173–74.

9 Axelrod, 174.

Chapter 3

1 Sophocles, *Antigone*, in *The Complete Greek Tragedies*, ed. David Grene and Richmond Lattimore (Chicago: University of Chicago Press, 1959), 2:170–71.

2 Exodus 32, *Schofield Reference Bible* (New York: Oxford University Press, 1927).

3 Cedric Whitman, *Homer and the Heroic Tradition* (New York: Norton, 1958), 199.

4 Whitman, 220.

5 Joseph Wood Krutch, *The Modern Temper: A Study and a Confession* (New York: Harcourt, Brace & World, 1956), 92.

6 Henrik Ibsen, *The Master Builder*, in *The Genius of the Scandinavian Theater*, ed. Evert Sprinchorn (New York: Mentor, 1956), 238.

7 Alain Robbe-Grillet, *For a New Novel*, trans. Richard Howard (New York: Grove Press, 1965), 57.

8 Robbe-Grillet, 72–73.

Chapter 4

1 References to *Hamlet* are to act, scene, and lines in the G. L. Kittredge edition of the play (New York and Boston: Ginn, 1967).

2 Harold Clarke Goddard, *The Meaning of Shakespeare* (Chicago: University of Chicago Press, 1951), 2:357.

3 Konrad Lorenz, *Studies in Animal and Human Behavior* (Cambridge: Harvard University Press, 1971), 2:357.

4 Irenaus Eibl-Eibesfeldt, *Ethology*, trans. Erich Klinghammer (New York: Holt, 1970), 315.

5 Goddard, 1:364.

6 Erik Erikson, "The Ontogeny of Ritualization in Man," *Philosophical Transactions of the Royal Society*, ser. B, 251, no. 722 (1966): 337–49.

7 Homer, *The Iliad of Homer*, trans. Richmond Lattimore (Chicago: University of Chicago Press, 1951), bk. 22, ll. 261–67.

8 Johann Wolfgang von Goethe, *Wilhelm Meister's Apprenticeship*, trans. Thomas Carlyle (London, 1851), bk. 4, chap. 13. (Original published in 1796.)

9 Konrad Lorenz, personal conversation. Tape recording in author's possession.

Chapter 5

1 *Works of Virgil*, trans. J. W. MacKail (New York: Random House, 1950), 267.

2 Virgil, 266.

3   *Satires of Juvenal*, trans. Rolfe Humphries (Bloomington: Indiana University Press, 1958), 42.

4   Boccaccio, *Decameron*, trans. Richard Aldington (New York: Dell, 1962), 32, 35.

5   Boccaccio, 173.

6   Boccaccio, 174.

7   Ebenezer Howard, *Garden Cities of To-morrow* (1898; reprint, Cambridge: MIT Press, 1965), 44.

8   Leo Marx, *The Machine in the Garden: Technology and the Pastoral Ideal in America* (New York: Oxford University Press, 1964), 141.

9   Thomas Jefferson, *Notes on the State of Virginia*, Query 19, quoted in Marx, 124.

10   Jefferson to William Short, November 28, 1814, quoted in Marx, 144.

11   Marx, 364.

12   *The Pleasaunte Historie of Lazarillo de Tormes*, trans. David Rowland (London, 1586), ed. J.E.V. Crofts (Oxford: Basil Blackwell, 1924), 11.

13   William Faulkner, *The Reivers* (New York: Random House, 1962), 121.

14   Johann von Grimmelshausen, *Simplicius Simplicissimus*, trans. George Schulz-Behrend (Indianapolis: Bobbs-Merrill, 1965), 27; further references are cited parenthetically in the text.

15   Joseph Heller, *Catch-22* (New York: Dell, 1955), 21; further references in text.

16   Thomas Mann, *Confessions of Felix Krull, Confidence Man*, trans. Denver Lindley (New York: Alfred Knopf, 1955), 13; further references in text.

Chapter 6

1   Karl von Frisch, *Animal Architecture* (New York: Harcourt, Brace Jovanovich, 1974), 31.

2   Steven Pinker, *The Language Instinct: How the Mind Creates Language* (New York: Harper, 1994), 18.

3   Frank Fraser Darling, *A Herd of Red Deer: A Study in Animal Behaviour* (London: Oxford University Press, 1937).

4   Joseph W. Meeker, *The Comedy of Survival: Studies in Literary Ecology* (New York: Charles Scribner's Sons, 1974).

5   E. O. Wilson, *Sociobiology: The New Synthesis* (Cambridge: Harvard University Press, 1975).

6   Richard Dawkins, *The Selfish Gene* (New York: Oxford University Press, 1976).

7   Robert Wright, *The Moral Animal: Why We Are the Way We Are* (New York: Vintage Books, 1994).

8   Wright, 8.

9   Wright, 5.

10   Wright, 314.

11   Richard Dawkins, *River Out of Eden: A Darwinian View of Life* (New York: Basic Books, 1995).

12   Dawkins, *River Out of Eden*, 83.

13   Paul Shepard, *Thinking Animals: Animals and the Development of Human Intelligence* (New York: Viking Press, 1978).

14   See note 2 to this chapter.

15   Pinker, 125.

16   Pinker, 409.

17   Donald E. Brown, *Human Universals* (New York: McGraw-Hill, 1991).

18   Quoted in Pinker, 413–15.

19   Pinker, 415.

20   E. O. Wilson, *On Human Nature* (Cambridge: Harvard University Press, 1979), and *Biophilia* (Cambridge: Harvard University Press, 1984); Stephen Kellert and E. O. Wilson, *The Biophilia Hypothesis* (Washington, D.C.: Island Press, 1993).

21   Donald R. Griffin, *Listening in the Dark: The Acoustic Orientation of Bats and Men* (New Haven: Yale University Press, 1958); *The Question of Animal Awareness: Evolutionary Continuity of Mental Experience*, rev. ed. (New York: Rockefeller University Press, 1981); introduction to *Animal Mind—Human Mind* (New York: Springer, 1982); *Animal Thinking* (Cambridge: Harvard University Press, 1984); and *Animal Minds* (Chicago: University of Chicago Press, 1992).

22   Griffin, *Animal Minds*, 258.

23   Griffin, *Animal Minds*, 259.

24   This speculation derives from personal communication between myself and Dr. Stuart Brown; based on research in progress.

25   Theodore Xenophon Barber, *The Human Nature of Birds* (New York: Penguin, 1993). Barber is a research psychologist and director of the Research Institute for Interdisciplinary Science in Boston.

26   Barber, 3.

27   Barber, 163.

28   Thomas Berry, *The Dream of the Earth* (San Francisco: Sierra Club Books, 1988), 124.

29   Brian Swimme and Thomas Berry, *The Universe Story: From the Primordial Flaring-Forth to the Ecozoic Era.* (San Francisco: HarperCollins, 1992).

30   Swimme and Berry, 246.

Chapter 7

1   Dante, Epistola 10, Letter to Can Grande della Scala, trans. P. H. Wickstead, in James H. Smith and Edd W. Parks, *The Great Critics* (New York: W. W. Norton, 1951), 148.

2   Dante Alighieri, *The Divine Comedy*, trans. Allen Mandelbaum (New York: Bantam Books, 1980), *Inferno*, 5.51.

3   Dante, *Inferno*, 9.5–6.

4   Dante, *Inferno*, 29.60–63.

5   Dante, *Inferno*, 31.37.

6   Dante, *Inferno*, 7.103.

7   Dante, *Inferno*, 18.106–8.

8   Dante, *Inferno*, 18.113–14.

9   Dante, *Inferno*, 1.31–50.

10   Dante, *Inferno*, 6.16–17.

11   Dante, *Inferno*, 13.13–14.

12   Dante, *Inferno*, 17.10–13.

13   Dante, *Inferno*, 17.9–10.

14   Dante, *Inferno*, 13.4–6.

15   Dante, *Inferno*, 22.143–44.

16   Dante, *Inferno*, 3.55–57.

17   Dante, *Inferno*, 3.18.

18   Dante, *Purgatorio*, 1.17–18.

19   Dante, *Purgatorio*, 13.2–3.

20   Dante, *Inferno*, 24.25–26.

21   Dante, *Purgatorio*, 10.46.

22   Dante, *Purgatorio*, 3.37.

23   Dante, *Purgatorio*, 27.142.

24   Dante, *Purgatorio*, 27.130–31.

25   Dante, *Purgatorio*, 18.19–20.

26 Dante, *Purgatorio*, 18.49–60.

27 Dante, *Purgatorio*, 17.91–96.

28 Dante, *Purgatorio*, 21.61–63.

29 Dante, *Purgatorio*, 28.2.

30 Dante, *Purgatorio*, 28.112–14.

31 Dante, *Purgatorio*, 28.119.

32 Dante, *Purgatorio*, 6.45.

33 Dante, *Paradiso*, 1.53–54.

34 Dante, *Paradiso*, 1.70.

35 Dante, *Paradiso*, 1.103–4.

36 Dante, *Paradiso*, 1.116–17.

37 Dante, *Paradiso*, 1.118–20.

38 Dante, *Paradiso*, 2.139.

39 Dante, *Paradiso*, 8.119.

40 Dante, *Paradiso*, 8.142–44.

41 Dante, *Paradiso*, 14.59–60.

42 Dante, *Paradiso*, 22.134–35.

43 Dante, *Paradiso*, 22.150.

44 Dante, *Paradiso*, 33.82–93.

45 Dante, *Paradiso*, 33.131.

46 Dante, *Paradiso*, 33.137–39.

47 Jacques Maritain, *Creative Intuition in Art and Poetry* (New York: Meridian, 1955), 264–81.

48 Dante, Epistola 10, in Smith and Parks, *The Great Critics*, p. 147.

Chapter 8

1 Barber, *Human Nature of Birds*, 171.

2 "Boids" is a program by Craig Reynolds of the Symbolics Graphics Division of Los Angeles. Reported in M. Mitchell Waldrop, *Complexity: The Emerging Science at the Edge of Order and Chaos* (New York: Simon & Schuster, 1994), 242–43. Reynolds maintains a World Wide Web site devoted to Boids, including demonstration versions of the program and links to various references, at http://reality.sgi.com/employees/craig/boids.html (as of mid-1997).

3 Wilson, *Sociobiology*, 161.

4 Fagen, *Animal Play Behavior*, 317.

Bibliography

Axelrod, Robert. *The Evolution of Cooperation*. New York: Basic Books, 1984.

Barber, Theodore Xenophon. *The Human Nature of Birds*. New York: Penguin, 1993.

Bateson, Gregory. *Steps to an Ecology of Mind*. New York: Ballantine Books, 1972.

————. *Mind and Nature: A Necessary Unity*. New York: E. P. Dutton, 1979.

Berry, Thomas. *The Dream of the Earth*. San Francisco: Sierra Club Books, 1988.

Boccaccio, *Decameron*. Trans. Richard Aldington. New York: Dell, 1962.

Brown, Donald E. *Human Universals*. New York: McGraw-Hill, 1991.

Buell, Lawrence. *The Environmental Imagination: Thoreau, Nature Writing, and the Formation of American Culture*. Cambridge: Harvard University Press, 1995.

Carse, James P. *Finite and Infinite Games: A Vision of Life as Play and Possibility*. New York: Ballantine Books, 1986.

Coles, Robert. *The Call of Stories: Teaching and the Moral Imagination*. Boston: Houghton Mifflin, 1989.

Dante Alighieri. *The Divine Comedy*. Trans. Allen Mandelbaum. New York: Bantam Books, 1980.

Darling, Frank Fraser. *A Herd of Red Deer: A Study in Animal Behaviour*. London: Oxford University Press, 1937.

Dawkins, Marion Stamp. *Through Our Eyes Only? The Search for Animal Consciousness*. New York: Oxford University Press, 1993.

Dawkins, Richard. *The Selfish Gene*. New York: Oxford University Press, 1976.

———. *River Out of Eden: A Darwinian View of Life*. New York: Basic Books, 1995.

Donaldson, O. Fred. *Playing by Heart*. Deerfield Beach, Fla.: Health Communications, 1993.

Eibl-Eibesfeldt, Irenaus. *Ethology*. Trans. Erich Klinghammer. New York: Holt, 1970.

Erikson, Eric. "The Ontogeny of Ritualization in Man." *Philosophical Transactions of the Royal Society*, ser. B, 251, no. 722 (1966): 147–526.

Estes, Clarissa Pinkola. *Women Who Run with the Wolves: Myths and Stories of the Wild Woman Archetype*. New York: Ballantine Books, 1992.

———. *The Gift of Story: A Wise Tale about What Is Enough*. New York: Ballantine Books, 1994.

Fagen, Robert. *Animal Play Behavior*. New York: Oxford University Press, 1981.

Faulkner, William. *The Reivers*. New York: Random House, 1962.

Frisch, Karl von. *Animal Architecture*. New York: Harcourt, Brace Jovanovich, 1974.

Glotfelty, Cheryll, and Harold Fromm. *The Ecocriticism Reader: Landmarks in Literary Ecology*. Athens: University of Georgia Press, 1996.

Goddard, Harold Clarke. *The Meaning of Shakespeare*. 2 vols. Chicago: University of Chicago Press, 1951.

Goethe, Johann Wolfgang von. *Wilhelm Meister's Apprenticeship*. Trans. Thomas Carlyle. London, 1851.

Gould, Stephen Jay. *Wonderful Life: The Burgess Shale and the Nature of History*. New York: Norton, 1989.

Griffin, Donald R. *Listening in the Dark: The Acoustic Orientation of Bats and Men*. New Haven: Yale University Press, 1958.

———. *The Question of Animal Awareness: Evolutionary Continuity of Mental Experience*. Rev. ed. New York: Rockefeller University Press, 1981.

———. Introduction to *Animal Mind—Human Mind*. New York: Springer, 1982.

———. *Animal Thinking*. Cambridge: Harvard University Press, 1984.

———. *Animal Minds*. Chicago: University of Chicago Press, 1992.

Grimmelshausen, Johann von. *Simplicius Simplicissimus*. Trans. George Schulz-Behrend. Indianapolis: Bobbs-Merrill, 1965.

Hayles, N. Katherine. *Chaos Bound: Orderly Disorder in Contemporary Literature and Science*. Ithaca: Cornell University Press, 1990.

Heller, Joseph. *Catch-22*. New York: Dell, 1955.

Homer. *The Iliad of Homer*. Trans. Richmond Lattimore. Chicago: University of Chicago Press, 1951.

Howard, Ebenezer. *Garden Cities of To-morrow*. 1898. Reprint, Cambridge: MIT Press, 1965.

Huizinga, Johan. *Homo Ludens: A Study of the Play Element in Culture*. Boston: Beacon Press, 1950.

Ibsen, Henrik. *The Master Builder*. In *The Genius of the Scandinavian Theater*, edited by Evert Sprinchorn. New York: Mentor, 1956.

Juvenal, *Satires*. Trans. Rolfe Humphries. Bloomington: Indiana University Press, 1958.

Kellert, Stephen and E. O. Wilson. *The Biophilia Hypothesis*. Washington, D.C.: Island Press, 1993.

Kroeber, Karl. *Ecological Literary Criticism: Romantic Imagining and the Biology of Mind*. New York: Columbia University Press, 1994.

Krutch, Joseph Wood. *The Modern Temper: A Study and a Confession*. New York: Harcourt, Brace and World, 1956.

Lorenz, Konrad. *Studies in Animal and Human Behavior*. 2 vols. Cambridge: Harvard University Press, 1971.

Mann, Thomas. *Confessions of Felix Krull, Confidence Man*. Trans. Denver Lindley. New York: Alfred Knopf, 1955.

Maritain, Jacques. *Creative Intuition in Art and Poetry*. New York: Meridian, 1955.

Marx, Leo. *The Machine in the Garden: Technology and the Pastoral Ideal in America*. New York: Oxford University Press, 1964.

Masson, Jeffrey M. *When Elephants Weep: The Emotional Lives of Animals*. New York: Delacorte Press, 1995.

Meeker, Joseph W. *The Comedy of Survival: Studies in Literary Ecology*. New York: Charles Scribner's Sons, 1974.

———. *The Comedy of Survival: In Search of an Environmental Ethic*. Los Angeles: Guild of Tutors Press, 1980.

Montague, Ashley. *Growing Young*. New York: Bergin and Garvey, 1981.

Nachmanovitch, Stephen. *Free Play: Improvisation in Life and Art*. Los Angeles: Jeremy P. Tarcher, 1990.

Oriard, Michael. *Sporting with the Gods: The Rhetoric of Play and Game in American Culture*. Cambridge: Cambridge University Press, 1983.

Penrose, Roger. *The Emperor's New Mind: Concerning Computers, Minds, and the Laws of Physics*. New York: Oxford University Press, 1989.

Pinker, Steven. *The Language Instinct: How the Mind Creates Language.* New York: Harper, 1994.

The Pleasaunte Historie of Lazarillo de Tormes. Trans. David Rowland (London, 1586). Ed. J.E.V. Crofts. Oxford: Basil Blackwell, 1924.

Roszak, Theodore. *The Voice of the Earth.* New York: Simon and Schuster, 1992.

Robbe-Grillet, Alain. *For a New Novel.* Trans. Richard Howard. New York: Grove Press, 1965.

Shepard, Paul. *Thinking Animals: Animals and the Development of Human Intelligence.* New York: Viking Press, 1978.

———. *The Others: How Animals Made Us Human.* Washington, D.C.: Island Press, 1996.

Smith, James H., and Edd W. Parks. *The Great Critics.* New York: W. W. Norton, 1951.

Sophocles. *Antigone.* In *The Complete Greek Tragedies,* edited by David Grene and Richmond Lattimore. Chicago: University of Chicago Press, 1959.

Spariosu, Mihai I. *Dionysus Reborn: Play and the Aesthetic Dimension in Modern Philosophical and Scientific Discourse.* Ithaca: Cornell University Press, 1989.

Sutton-Smith, Brian. *Play and Learning.* New York: Gardner Press, 1979.

Swimme, Brian, and Thomas Berry. *The Universe Story: From the Primordial Flaring-Forth to the Ecozoic Era.* San Francisco: HarperCollins, 1992.

Virgil. *Works of Virgil.* Trans. J. W. MacKail. New York: Random House, 1950.

Waldrop, M. Mitchell. *Complexity: The Emerging Science at the Edge of Order and Chaos.* New York: Simon and Schuster, 1994.

Weiner, Jonathan. *The Beak of the Finch: A Story of Evolution in Our Time.* New York: Alfred Knopf, 1994.

Whitman, Cedric. *Homer and the Heroic Tradition.* New York: Norton, 1958.

Wilber, Ken. *Sex, Ecology, and Spirituality: The Spirit of Evolution.* Boston: Shambhala Press, 1995.

Wilson, E. O. *Sociobiology: The New Synthesis.* Cambridge: Harvard University Press, 1975.

———. *On Human Nature.* Cambridge: Harvard University Press, 1979.

———. *Biophilia.* Cambridge: Harvard University Press, 1984.

Wright, Robert. *The Moral Animal: Why We Are the Way We Are.* New York: Vintage Books, 1994.

Index

tragi-comedy, 34
Twelfth Night (Shakespeare), 15

universals, human, 88
universities, 8

Virgil, and pastoral, 51–52, 73;
    Dante's, 94–95
vitamin effect, 115

Waldrop, M. Mitchell, 113
Whitman, Cedric, 29–30
whooping cranes, 4
wilderness, 19, 51, 57–59, 61; pica-
    resque, 72
Wilson, Edward O., 78, 82
work ethic, 35
Wright, Robert, 78–80

About the Author

Joseph W. Meeker is a human ecologist with a Ph.D. in comparative literature, and master's and postdoctoral studies in wildlife ecology and comparative animal and human behavior. He has been a ranger and field ecologist in the National Park Service in Alaska, Oregon, and California. He has been a broadcaster on radio and television in Canada and the United States. He produced and hosted the radio series "Minding the Earth" carried on many National Public Radio stations during the 1980s. He has taught at the University of California and the University of Alaska, and is currently a Core Faculty member at the Graduate School of the Union Institute. His books include *Spheres of Life*, *The Comedy of Survival*, and *Minding the Earth*.

Dr. Meeker lives with his wife on a forested island in Puget Sound near Seattle. His research into comedy and play is an exploration of the relationships between humanity and the natural world. His work seeks to bring science, literature, and philosophy together for a more comprehensive and friendly understanding of the meaning and dynamics of living systems.